MW00389627

Channel Analysis

The Key to
Share Price Prediction

Second Edition

Other titles in the *Millard on . . .* Series

Channel Analysis

The Key to
Share Price Prediction

Second Edition

Brian J. Millard

JOHN WILEY & SONS

Chichester • New York • Weinheim • Brisbane • Singapore • Toronto

First edition published by Qudos Publications, 1989

This edition copyright © 1997 by John Wiley & Sons Ltd,
Baffins Lane, Chichester,
West Sussex PO19 1UD, England

National   01243 779777
International (+44) 1243 779777
e-mail (for orders and customer service enquiries):
cs-books@wiley.co.uk
Visit our Home Page on http://www.wiley.co.uk
or http://www.wiley.com

All Rights Reserved. No part of this book may be reproduced, stored in a retrieval system, or transmitted, in any form or by any means, electronic, mechanical, photocopying, recording, scanning or otherwise, except under the terms of the Copyright, Designs and Patents Act 1988 or under the terms of a licence issued by the Copyright Licensing Agency, 90 Tottenham Court Road, London W1P 9HE, UK, without the permission in writing of John Wiley and Sons Ltd, Baffins Lane, Chichester, West Sussex, UK PO19 1UD.

Other Wiley Editorial Offices

John Wiley & Sons, Inc., 605 Third Avenue,
New York, NY 10158-0012, USA

WILEY-VCH Verlag GmbH,
Pappelallee 3, D-69469 Weinheim, Germany

Jacaranda Wiley Ltd, 33 Park Road, Milton,
Queensland 4064, Australia

John Wiley & Sons (Asia) Pte Ltd, 2 Clementi Loop #02-01,
Jin Xing Distripark, Singapore 129809

John Wiley & Sons (Canada) Ltd, 22 Worcester Road,
Rexdale, Ontario M9W 1L1, Canada

Library of Congress Cataloging-in-Publication Data

Millard, Brian J.
    Channel analysis : the key to share price prediction / Brian J.
Millard. — 2nd ed.
      p. cm. — (Millard on — series)
    Includes bibliographical references and index.
    ISBN 0-471-96845-5 (pbk.)
    1. Stock price forecasting. 2. Investment analysis. 3. Portfolio
management. I. Title. II. Series: Millard, Brian J. Millard on —
series.
HG4637.M55   1997
332.63'222'042—dc21   96–46490
                                                CIP

British Library Cataloguing in Publication Data

A catalogue record for this book is available from the British Library

ISBN 0-471-96845-5

Typeset in 10.5/12pt Times by Dorwyn Ltd, Rowlands Castle, Hants
Printed and bound in Great Britain by Redwood Books, Trowbridge, Wiltshire
This book is printed on acid-free paper responsibly manufactured from sustainable forestation, for which at least two trees are planted for each one used for paper production.

Contents

Preface to this Edition

Since *Channel Analysis* was first published in 1989 the technique is now widely used by private and institutional investors. It has become recognised as an excellent method for improving the timing of investments, thereby reducing risk to a minimum. It appeals to the small private investor who does not use a computer, but is content to draw charts and channels manually. It also appeals to the computerised investor, since software programs are available to carry out the channel calculations automatically.

Whichever method, manual or computer, is used by the investor, stress is once again placed on a totally disciplined approach as being the only way to make and hold on to profits. It is only through discipline that the investor ignores the inner voice that says that a falling share price will turn around if only more time is allowed. It is only through discipline that an investor avoids jumping in too early before a buying signal is confirmed. It is only through discipline that an investor ignores the torrent of investment advice in the press.

The availability of software programs has made it easy to investigate the various cycles present in share price data, and this topic is addressed rather more fully than in the first edition. Finally, it is shown how the powerful technique of probability analysis greatly improves the estimation of channel turning points, thereby increasing the profit potential considerably.

Brian J. Millard
Bramhall

Preface to the First Edition

In my previous book *Stocks and Shares Simplified* I just touched on the underlying principles by which the future course of share prices could be estimated by means of boundaries based on long term moving averages. I then became aware of the work of J. M. Hurst in the United States, and came to realise that we were both heading in the same direction by slightly different routes. These two approaches have been combined in the technique of Channel Analysis, and readers of this book will soon begin to see that this is the most powerful technique available for predicting the direction of share prices over the near future.

The book does not claim 100% success in predicting price movement, since a considerable proportion of price movement is random and therefore not predictable. Where the book does claim success is in determining the status of the various cycles present in share price data. This knowledge is of paramount importance in identifying buying and selling points only a short time after they occur. This reduces the risk to the investor while giving him a large proportion of the subsequent gain made by the share price.

The book also shows that the policy of buying a share and then holding on to it through thick and thin is a flawed one, and that much greater profits can be made by trading on a short term basis even when dealing costs are taken into account.

Finally the importance of a disciplined approach to investment is stressed, enabling the investor to hold on to the profits which he has made.

October 1989

Brian J. Millard
Bramhall

1

Buy and Hold?

There has always been a difference of opinion between those investors who believe that the best policy is to buy a share and then virtually forget it and those investors who believe that better profits can be made by constant forays in and out of the market. Market professionals obviously belong to the latter category, since they appear to spend their whole day engaged in buying and selling operations. During the privatisations of British Telecom, British Gas, the water and electricity companies, etc., many amateur investors came to the conclusion that the best profit was the quick profit that could be made by selling the shares within a few days of issue, and therefore they took the same view as the professionals. However, if we look at the vast majority of investors in the privatisation issues, we find that they have no clear objective. They firmly believe that the share price will rise consistently over the foreseeable future, and have no inclination to sell unless sudden demands for capital are made on them. In other words, for most of these investors, their selling action will be dictated by personal circumstances and not the behaviour of the share price itself.

This view of buying shares and then holding on to them for long periods of time has much to commend it: it makes no demands on the investor in terms of having to manage the various shares that go to make up the investor's portfolio, and it has resulted in good profits for most of the quality shares over the last 15 years or so. Looking at this statement more closely will lead to the conclusion that this buy and hold policy makes no demands on the investor simply because good profits have been made in most shares. If shares had been much more mixed in their long term performance then it would have been necessary for investors to have taken a much more active stance. The fallacy in most investors' reasoning is therefore that share prices will inexorably rise in the future if a long term, say 10- or 15-year view, is taken. This long term view can even accommodate drastic crashes in the market such as occurred in October 1987. On this long term view, most falls in the market can be accepted merely as blips in the steady upwards progress, the October crash being just a slightly larger blip than has been the norm since 1929. We shall see later in the discussion on cycles in the market that the rise we have seen over the last 15 years cannot continue for ever, and that once the very long term cycles start to reach their peaks, then the long term rise will turn into a long term fall.

GAINS AND COMPOUND GAINS

Before we can proceed any further with a discussion of the merits of different investment strategies, we have to get clear in our minds the various ways in which we can calculate and compare gains (or losses) in investment capital. The most common way of calculating a gain is to express it as a percentage change from the starting value. Thus if an investor starts with £1000 and turns it into £2000 over a certain period of time then quite obviously he has made a gain of 100%. A different way of expressing the gain is to consider it as a factor by which the starting amount has to be multiplied. In this present example the investor has doubled his money, and therefore the gain factor is 2. If we deal with numbers that are not so round, then for example an investor turning £1000 into £1450 over a period of time will have made a gain of 45%, while the gain factor is 1.45. In this chapter we will be using both gain factors and percentage gains. It is easy to convert from percentages to gain factors and vice versa by the simple formulas:

$$\text{Gain factor} = (100 + \text{percentage gain})/100$$

and

$$\text{percentage gain} = 100 \times (\text{gain factor} - 1)$$

Now, of course, a gain in capital becomes meaningless without a time-scale attached to it. An investor A who makes 100% on his starting capital over five years has not done as well as an investor B who makes the same gain in four years. The best way of comparing the two performances is to express them as gains (either gain factors or percentage gains will do) over the same time period, which in this case would conveniently be a year. One simple way of doing this would be to divide the total gain by the number of years. We would then find that investor A who doubled his money over five years would have made a gain of 20% per annum and investor B who took four years to do this would have made a gain of 25% per annum. The disadvantage of calculating gains in this way is that it ignores the ability to compound gains, i.e. to plough back into the next investment the total proceeds from the previous investment, both the original stake and any gain made from it. Throughout this chapter we will be adopting this approach of calculating gains as compound gains, i.e. as if they were made annually and reinvested.

Although such compound gains can be calculated from the percentage gain made each year, it is much easier to calculate them if we use gain factors, since we simply multiply the gain factors together to get the overall gain.

As an example, if we make a gain of 11% per annum, then this is the same as a gain factor of 1.11. To compute the gain over a number of years, say five, we simply multiply the gain factors together the number of times that we have years.

Thus 1.11 compounded for five years = $1.11 \times 1.11 \times 1.11 \times 1.11 \times 1.11$

$$= (1.11)^5$$

$$= 1.685$$

By our formula above, a gain factor of 1.685 is a percentage gain of 68.5% over five years. Note the difficulty of calculating the above if we tried to use percentages instead of gain factors. Scientific and financial calculators have a key which is usually labelled x^y which makes this calculation easier than multiplying the numbers together the requisite number of times. In this case x is the gain factor, e.g. 1.11, and y is the number of years.

If the gains differ for each of the five years, then we still use the above method, but replace the value of 1.11 for that year by the appropriate gain factor. We cannot then use the x^y key on the calculator, of course, since the x values are not all the same.

On a computer using BASIC, the line which gives the compounded gain, say G, from the annual gain, say A, is:

$$G = A \wedge Y$$

where Y is the number of years.

Having shown how to compute an annual gain into a five-year gain, for example, we have to do the reverse of this to express the five-year gains of investors A and B as annual gains. Each of them made gains of 100%, i.e. gain factors of 2.0. Thus,

$$\text{annual gain} = \text{5th root of 2.0 for investor A}$$

$$= 1.149$$

$$\text{annual gain} = \text{4th root of 2.00 for investor B}$$

$$= 1.189$$

Thus if the gain is known for an n-year period, the annual gain is the nth root of this n-year gain. The problem with reducing a gain to a gain over a shorter time period is that most simple calculators only have square roots, and not nth roots. Some financial and all scientific calculators will have this facility, which is performed by a key which is usually labelled $x^{1/y}$. In this case, x is the overall gain factor and y would be the number of years, or whichever period it is desired to reduce the gain to. With a computer, to get the annual gain A from a gain of G which has been obtained over a period of Y years is a one-line program in BASIC using the EXP and LOG functions:

$$A = EXP(LOG(G)/Y)$$

BUY AND HOLD FOR A LONG TERM

The correctness of the buy and hold strategy can appear to be confirmed by a chart of just about all shares that have been quoted for a 15-year period on the London stock market. As just one example, the chart of Grand Metropolitan is shown in Figure 1.1. Taking the extremes of the chart, an investor could have bought Grand Met shares at 52p on 6th January 1978 and sold them on 31st January 1995 at 464p. If dealing costs are ignored, this represents a profit of 412p per share, i.e. a profit of 792% on the initial price.

Unfortunately, dealing costs cannot be ignored, and the small investor suffers more than most as far as the level of costs is concerned. For the sake of argument, if we assume that a parcel of 1000 shares was purchased at 52p, then the dealing costs on such an amount would be approximately 2.5%. The selling costs would be approximately 1.5%. These percentages increase rapidly as the value of the deal falls below £1000 and decrease only slowly as the deal moves into the tens of thousands of pounds.

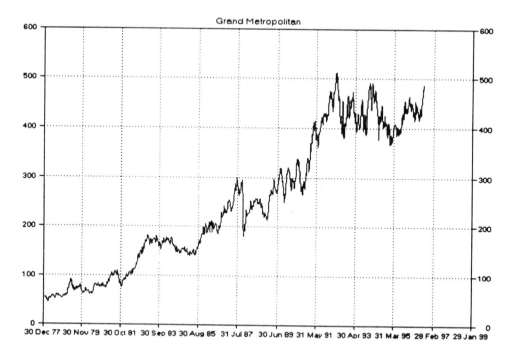

Figure 1.1 The Grand Metropolitan share price since 1978

Thus the dealing costs of buying 1000 shares at 52p would be about £13 and the selling costs of selling at 464p would be about £69. Now we can calculate a more realistic profit for the entire deal than the 792% we noted above:

Buy 1000 shares @ 52p   Outlay = £520 + £13 = £533
Sell 1000 shares @ 464p   Receipts = £4640 – £69 = £4571

Actual gain = £4038

This represents a gain of 757% on the outlay of £533. Therefore the dealing costs of this transaction have reduced the overall gain by some 35% over the 18-year period.

If we are going to make this a realistic exercise, then there is one important aspect that is missing from this calculation. This concerns the dividends that would have been paid during the 18-year period for which the shares would have been held. To simplify matters, we can consider that Grand Metropolitan consistently paid a 5% dividend, year in and year out over this period.

Since the average share price was halfway between 52p and 464p, i.e. 258p, we can estimate the cumulative dividend as:

$$18 \times 1000 \times 258p \times 5\% = £2322$$

This increases the actual gain from £4250 as calculated without dividends to £6572 with dividends. This now gives a gain of 1233% on the initial outlay of £533.

Since we require some standard timescale over which to compare the gain from one situation with the gain from another, it is best to state this gain from investment in Grand Metropolitan shares as a percentage gain per annum. As we discussed above, it is not correct simply to divide the 1233% by 18 and use this as the annual gain. The annual gain has to be such that it compounds into a gain of 1233% over the 18-year period, so that we could compare it with that made by an investor who leaves his money and the accumulated interest in an interest-bearing account. If we do this, we find that the gain of 1233% equates to a gain of 15.5% per annum. This is superior to any gain that could have been made by depositing the money in the money market for one-year periods, year in and year out, and so appears to verify that long term investment in shares is an excellent strategy.

The profit from the position is made because the share price has risen more than sufficiently to offset the buying and selling costs and we have had the advantage of a number of dividends over the time period.

MULTIPLE TRANSACTIONS OVER A LONG TERM

The alternative to buying shares and holding them for long periods of time is to buy and sell them over shorter time periods. We still have to satisfy

Table 1.1 Yearly starting values, ending values and gains/
losses made in the Grand Metropolitan share price from 1978
to 1995

Year	Start price	End price	% gain/loss
1978	52	57	9.6
1979	56	62.5	11.6
1980	63.5	76.5	20.5
1981	76	88	15.8
1982	93	162.5	74.7
1983	170.5	165	−3.2
1984	167.5	157.5	−5.9
1985	149	199	33.5
1986	205.5	229	11.4
1987	228.5	233.5	2.2
1988	224.5	215	−4.2
1989	221.5	314	41.8
1990	319	338.5	6.1
1991	337.5	428	26.8
1992	449	459	2.2
1993	465	475.5	2.2
1994	484	407	−15.9
1995	404.5	464	14.7

the above criterion, i.e. that the price rise over the shorter timescale will be
more than sufficient to offset the buying and selling costs. Whether we will
still have the advantage of any dividends will depend upon the time period
over which we hold the shares. If we are lucky, then holding the shares for
just one day could capture a dividend.

It is interesting to view Grand Met shares in terms of their yearly
performance since the beginning of 1978, i.e. look at the gain or loss that
occurred over each calendar year since that time. These annual changes
are shown in Table 1.1.

We can see that out of these 18 yearly changes, seven were either losses,
or gains of only 2.2%. Thus, there is no question that if we had not been
invested in Grand Met during those seven years, but had found a better
home in the money market for our funds, then even taking into account
the dealing costs involved in selling and buying back a year later we would
have made a much better return over the whole 18-year period.

Ignoring the price movement in the shares themselves over any particular time period, the major disadvantages of such a strategy of buying and
selling frequently would appear to be:

• We have to carry buying costs of 2.5% and selling costs of 1.5% with
  each buying and selling transaction. A switching from one share to
  another therefore is an expensive operation.

• We have to spend time managing our portfolio.

The second of these disadvantages should be ignored by any serious investor. If the reward becomes high enough through the application of a

successful investment strategy, then the time spent is worthwhile. The only negative aspect therefore is the high dealing cost of carrying out a strategy of buying and selling at frequent intervals.

The success of such a strategy now depends upon the answers to just three questions:

- Do prices rise sufficiently over the investment term to offset the transaction costs and generate profit?
- Since profits will be compounded, and bearing in mind the transaction costs, what is the shortest practicable time period over which to hold a share in order to maximise profits?
- How difficult is it to capture good price rises and avoid bad price falls in a given time period?

In this chapter we will look at these first two questions. The objective of this book as a whole is to answer the third question.

Before any transaction can generate a profit, the price rise over the period of that transaction has to be considerably in excess of 5% in order comfortably to clear the dealing costs. A logical approach to this question of multiple transactions is to investigate shorter and shorter time periods over which the shares are held in order to decide at what point the average gain per transaction falls below that necessary to make a profit, i.e. falls below say 5%. There will come a point at which no profit will be made, and so we can say that shortening the timescale would appear to be working against us as far as the level of profit is concerned.

On the other hand, as we fit more and more transactions into a certain time period and reinvest the total proceeds of one transaction into the next, the compounding effect will move in our favour, increasing profits dramatically. Thus we expect that:

1. Reducing the transaction time reduces the real gain per transaction.
2. Reducing the transaction time increases the compound gain of multiple transactions.

The exercise therefore comes down to an investigation of the combined effect of these two factors which are acting in opposite directions. A staged approach to this question is valuable in helping us to gain an insight into the relationship between these two factors for a typical share such as Grand Metropolitan.

There is a third point to be made here, and that concerns the rate of gain. Thus although the reduced transaction time should reduce the gain made per transaction, then since this occurs over a shorter timescale the rate of gain expressed, say, as a rate per week may be much better than that made from an investment with a longer transaction period. This is apart from any advantage to be obtained by compounding successive gains.

Looking at the Grand Met share price in Figure 1.1 again, we can see some upward surges in share price which make good gains over time

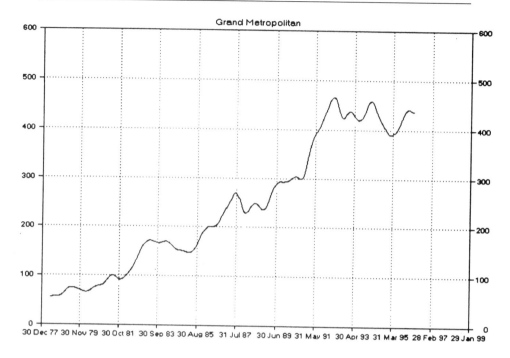

Figure 1.2 Medium term trends in the Grand Metropolitan share price since 1978. These are represented by a centred 41-week moving average

periods of up to about two years. These trends are displayed in Figure 1.2, and have been isolated by using a centred 41-week moving average as discussed in Chapter 3. Taking the rising part of the trends only, there are 13 such uptrends in the figure. In this chapter we are concerned only with the share prices at the time the trends started and when they finished. The beginning and end of a trend is signified by the changes in direction of the average.

The share prices at the turning points in these 13 uptrends are given in Table 1.2. The timescale of these trends varies from 16 weeks up to 84 weeks with an average time of 45 weeks, i.e. nearly one year from the beginning to the end of the average trend. Note that the longest trend, 84 weeks, gave the largest gain, but one of the two shortest trends of 16 weeks did not give the smallest gain. In other words there is no obvious direct relationship between the length of time of an uptrend and the rise that occurs during it. The average gain for these 13 trends was 43.6%, corresponding to a gain factor of 1.436.

We are, in the present exercise, trying to compare the performance of an investor who bought and held Grand Met shares for 18 years with one who took advantage of these 13 trends, buying at the start of each trend and selling at the end of that trend. In order to do this we have to adjust the

Table 1.2 Starting values, ending values and gains made in 13 upward trends in the Grand Metropolitan share price from 1978 to 1995

Start date	Start price	End date	End price	Gain	% gain	Gain factor
10 Mar 78	44	15 Jun 79	70	26	59.1	1.59
07 Mar 80	67	19 Jun 81	102	35	52.2	1.52
06 Nov 81	75.5	06 May 83	164	88.5	117.2	2.17
21 Oct 83	153.5	10 Feb 84	174	20.5	13.4	1.13
26 Apr 85	142.5	04 Apr 86	209	66.5	46.7	1.47
11 Jul 86	194	26 Jun 87	272.5	78.5	40.5	1.41
01 Jan 88	224.5	17 Jun 88	256.25	31.75	14.1	1.14
18 Nov 88	228.5	08 Sep 89	317	88.5	38.7	1.39
02 Mar 90	273.5	22 Jun 90	337	63.5	23.2	1.23
28 Sep 90	266	08 May 92	510	244	91.7	1.92
09 Oct 92	380	19 Mar 93	472	92	24.2	1.24
09 Jul 93	408	14 Jan 94	491	83	20.3	1.20
17 Feb 95	368	29 Dec 95	464	96	26.1	1.26
Averages				78	43.6	1.436

performance of each investor to the same time period. This can be done in several ways:

1. Adjust the gain from the seven transactions over 45 weeks to a gain over 18 years, i.e. 936 weeks.
2. Adjust the gain from the one transaction over 936 weeks down to a gain over 45 weeks.
3. Adjust both gains to some other common time period, e.g. one week.

Although at this point option 3 gives us twice as much work to do as options 1 or 2, adjusting the gains from both types of investment to an equivalent gain over one week will have the advantage that we will be able to compare other transactions over other time periods to this same common standard, giving a more realistic comparison between them.

Taking the long term investor first, the gain factor of 8.92 over 18 years (936 weeks) will reduce down to an annual gain of the 18th root of 8.92, which is a gain factor of 1.129 271 per annum. This is a gain in percentage terms of 12.9% per annum.

Brought to a weekly basis, the weekly gain is the 936th root of 8.92, which is 1.002 341 over one week. In percentage terms, this is equivalent to 0.2341% per week. This is the gain that, if reinvested each year, would compound to a gain factor of 8.92, or 792%, over 936 weeks.

Carrying out the same calculation for the investor who buys and sells with the 13 trends with an average gain of 1.436 over 45 weeks, we have to raise 1.436 to the power (52/45) which gives an annual gain factor of 1.519. In percentage terms this is equivalent to 51.9% per annum. This is the gain that if reinvested each year for 18 years will give an ultimate gain of 1.436, i.e. 43.6%.

Compared on an annual basis, therefore, and with the important proviso that **dealing costs are ignored**, the gain from taking advantage of 13 upward surges in the share price over the 18-year period rather than one such surge lasting 18 years improves the gain on an annual basis from 12.9% to 51.9%, i.e. by a factor of about four.

Because dealing costs are high, they will have a considerable influence on profit as we increase the number of transactions that take place in a given time period, and therefore we have to take them into account when computing the various possibilities which we wish to compare. The buying and selling prices given in Table 1.1 have to be adjusted for these costs if we are to get a realistic idea of the gains which would be made from these seven transactions. To do this we adjust the buying price upwards by the typical amount of a buying cost, say 2.5%, and adjust the selling price downwards by the amount of these selling costs, say 1.5%. These details are given in Table 1.3. The effect of these costs is to reduce the average gain per transaction from 43.6% down to 38.05%.

Taking the long term investor first, the adjusted gain factor of 8.57 over 18 years (936 weeks) will reduce down to an annual gain of the 18th root of 8.57, which is a gain factor of 1.126 762 per annum. This is a gain in percentage terms of 12.67% per annum.

Brought to a weekly basis, the weekly gain is the 936th root of 8.57, which is 1.002 298 over one week. In percentage terms, this is equivalent to 0.2298% per week. This is the gain that, if reinvested each year, would compound to a gain factor of 8.57, or 757%, over 936 weeks.

Table 1.3 Buying prices, selling prices and gains in the 13 major trends in the Grand Metropolitan share price adjusted for dealing costs

Buy price	Sell price	Gain	Real B.P.	Real S.P.	Real gain	% gain
44	70	26	45.1	68.95	23.85	52.9
67	102	35	68.68	100.47	31.79	46.29
75.5	164	88.5	77.39	161.54	84.15	108.73
153.5	174	20.5	157.3	171.39	14.09	8.96
142.5	209	66.5	146.1	205.87	59.77	40.91
194	272.5	78.5	198.85	268.4	69.55	34.97
224.5	256.25	31.75	230.11	252.41	22.3	9.69
228.5	317	88.5	234.21	312.25	78.04	33.32
273.5	337	63.5	280.33	331.95	51.62	18.41
266	510	244	272.65	502.35	229.7	84.25
380	472	92	389.5	464.92	75.42	19.36
408	491	83	418.2	483.64	65.44	15.64
368	464	96	377.2	457.04	79.84	21.17
Averages		78			68.12	38.05

Carrying out the same calculation for the investor who buys and sells with the 13 trends with an average adjusted gain of 1.381 over 45 weeks, we have to raise 1.381 to the power (52/45) which gives an annual gain factor of 1.452. In percentage terms this is equivalent to 45.2% per annum. This is the gain that if reinvested each year for 18 years will give an ultimate gain of 1.381, i.e. 38.1%.

Compared on an annual basis, therefore, and **with dealing costs now being taken into account**, the gain from taking advantage of 13 upward surges in the share price over the 18-year period rather than one such surge lasting 18 years **improves the gain on an annual basis from 12.67% to 45.2%**, i.e. by a factor of about three and a half.

The clear message so far is that the theoretical annual rate of gain made from shorter term transactions is vastly superior to the rate of gain made by buying and holding.

The reason we use the word theoretical is because we have made the assumption that we buy at the exact beginning of a trend and sell at the exact end. We shall take a more realistic view of where an investor might have got on board a rising trend, and where he would get off it, later in this chapter. At the moment we are simply trying to evaluate the theoretical effect of increasing the number of transactions over a certain time period. The reason, of course, that these 13 transactions give a superior gain is because the perfect timing of our theoretical investor takes him out of the market while the price is falling, whereas the buy and hold investor has to cope with the ups and downs of the 18-year period.

Looking at Figure 1.1 more clearly, we can see that as well as the medium term trends we have been analysing so far, there are trends of a shorter timescale. These trends are isolated by means of a five-week average, shown in Figure 1.3. The share prices at the turning points can be extracted just as in Figure 1.2 in order to analyse the price changes caused by these short term trends. There are 41 such short term uptrends, and the price data for these are given in Table 1.4. These trends lasted for an average of 12 weeks, as opposed to the 45 weeks of the longer term trends. The average rise of each of these 12-week trends was 22.7%.

Just as in the case of the 13 longer term trends, we have to adjust the buying and selling points of the trends to allow for buying and selling costs. This is done in Table 1.5. We find that the average gain per transaction now falls to 17.94%. In order to compare this gain over a 12-week period with the previous values for 18 years and 45 weeks, we have to recalculate the gain as if it occurred over one year. We find that the gain factor of 1.1794 over 12 weeks is equivalent to a gain factor of 2.044 per annum, i.e. 104.4% per annum. This value supports our view that the rate of gain increases as we shorten the transaction time, even though of course the gain per transaction is less.

Since we have this rate of gain moving so positively in our favour, the natural next step is to look for even shorter uptrends to take advantage of

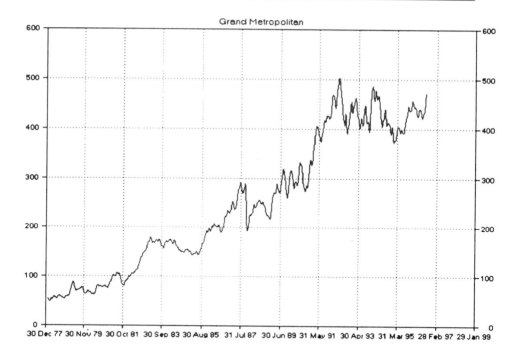

Figure 1.3   Short term trends in the Grand Metropolitan share price since 1978. These are represented by a centred five-week moving average

in this way. In Figure 1.4 we show an expanded portion of the Grand Met chart between July 1984 and September 1987. The very short term movements which could not be seen clearly in Figure 1.1 can now be seen easily. In this time period there are 34 such trends. The actual price movements for these 34 trends are given in Table 1.6. Many of these trends last for only one week, and the longest for eight weeks. The average length of time for which these very short term trends persist is 2.6 weeks. The average gain of these 34 transactions is 7.9% compared with the 22.7% in Table 1.4. We now appear to be coming to the shortest possible trends which will give us a profit, since we still have to adjust these for the dealing costs.

This is done in Table 1.7, once again by increasing the buying prices by 2.5% and decreasing the selling prices by 1.5%. Now we can see that the average gain per transaction has fallen to 3.7%. Once again, in order to compare with the previous calculations, we have to express this gain as if it occurred over one year.

As before, we have to upgrade this gain to the equivalent gain over a one-year period, and this works out as a gain factor of 2.068, or 106.8% per annum. Since this is only marginally higher than the rate of 104.4% per annum obtained with the 41 short term trends of Tables 1.4 and 1.5, it would appear that we are at about the optimum number of trades over the

Table 1.4 Gains made in short term trends in the Grand Metropolitan share price

Date	Price	Date	Price	Weeks	Rise	% rise	Factor
03 Mar 78	45.75	26 May 78	56.5	11	10.75	23.5	1.235
07 Jul 78	52	11 Aug 78	58.5	5	6.5	12.5	1.125
17 Nov 78	51.75	02 Feb 79	57.25	9	5.5	10.6	1.106
16 Feb 79	57.75	20 Apr 79	89.75	9	32	55.4	1.554
06 Jul 79	68.5	05 Oct 79	77	13	8.5	12.4	1.124
07 Dec 79	64.5	25 Jan 80	72	7	7.5	11.6	1.116
23 May 80	60	18 Jul 80	81.5	8	21.5	35.8	1.358
10 Oct 80	75.5	28 Nov 80	83	7	7.5	9.9	1.099
16 Jan 81	73	01 May 81	104.5	16	31.5	43.1	1.431
29 May 81	98	03 Jul 81	108.5	5	10.5	10.7	1.107
30 Oct 81	76.5	18 Feb 83	181	68	104.5	136.6	2.366
13 May 83	164	29 Jul 83	179.5	11	15.5	9.4	1.094
14 Oct 83	151.5	09 Dec 83	175.5	8	24	15.8	1.158
30 Dec 83	165	27 Jan 84	176.5	4	11.5	6.9	1.069
06 Apr 84	162	04 May 84	177	4	15	9.2	1.092
28 Sep 84	144	09 Nov 84	152.5	6	8.5	5.9	1.059
22 Mar 85	141.5	31 May 85	152.5	10	11	7.7	1.077
28 Jun 85	141	22 Nov 85	198	21	57	40.4	1.404
06 Dec 85	183	03 Jan 86	205.5	4	22.5	12.3	1.123
24 Jan 86	186.5	11 Apr 86	211.5	11	25	13.4	1.134
08 Aug 86	185	28 Nov 86	241	16	56	30.2	1.302
16 Jan 87	227	27 Feb 87	254	6	27	11.8	1.118
03 Apr 87	229	17 Jul 87	295	16	66	28.8	1.288
21 Aug 87	263	09 Oct 87	293.5	7	30.5	11.6	1.116
13 Nov 87	192	11 Mar 88	244.5	17	52.5	27.3	1.273
23 Dec 88	213	05 May 89	296.25	19	83.25	39.1	1.391
16 Jun 89	267	25 Aug 89	318	10	51	19.1	1.191
27 Oct 89	249	05 Jan 90	319	10	70	28.1	1.281
27 Apr 90	277	22 Jun 90	337	8	60	21.7	1.217
21 Sep 90	266	04 Jan 91	337.5	15	71.5	26.9	1.269
25 Jan 91	311.5	03 May 91	413.5	14	102	32.7	1.327
28 Jun 91	360	25 Oct 91	423	17	63	17.5	1.175
29 Nov 91	412	31 Jan 92	471	9	59	14.3	1.143
20 Mar 92	434	29 May 92	511	10	77	17.7	1.177
09 Oct 92	380	21 Jan 93	465	12	85	22.4	1.224
28 May 93	392	27 Aug 93	457	13	65	16.6	1.166
12 Nov 93	386	14 Jan 94	491	9	105	27.2	1.272
24 Jun 94	376	26 Aug 94	445	9	69	18.4	1.184
20 Jan 95	366	21 Apr 95	408	13	42	11.5	1.115
30 Jun 95	385.5	13 Oct 95	454	15	68.5	17.8	1.178
03 Nov 95	432	29 Dec 95	464	8	32	7.4	1.074
Averages				11.9	43.2	22.7	

18-year period in terms of rate of gain per week. However, bearing in mind the additional effort required for these very short term transactions, we can consider that using the short term trends rather than the very short term trends represents the optimum, and its annual gain of 104.4% is a

Table 1.5 Buying prices, selling prices and gains in short term trends in the Grand Metropolitan share price adjusted for dealing costs

Buy price	Sell price	Gain	Real B.P.	Real S.P.	Real gain	% gain
45.75	56.5	10.75	46.9	55.65	8.75	18.66
52	58.5	6.5	53.3	57.62	4.32	8.11
51.75	57.25	5.5	53.04	56.4	3.36	6.33
57.75	89.75	32	59.19	88.4	29.21	49.35
68.5	77	8.5	70.2	75.85	5.65	8.04
64.5	72	7.5	66.1	70.92	4.82	7.29
60	81.5	21.5	61.5	80.28	18.78	30.54
75.5	83	7.5	77.4	81.76	4.36	5.62
73	104.5	31.5	74.8	102.93	28.13	37.61
98	108.5	10.5	100.45	106.87	6.42	6.39
76.5	181	104.5	78.42	178.28	99.86	127.35
164	179.5	15.5	168.1	176.8	8.7	5.18
151.5	175.5	24	155.29	172.87	17.58	11.31
165	176.5	11.5	169.13	173.85	4.72	2.79
162	177	15	166.05	174.35	8.3	5.0
144	152.5	8.5	147.6	150.21	2.61	1.77
141.5	152.5	11	145.0	150.21	5.21	3.59
141	198	57	144.53	195.03	50.5	34.94
183	205.5	22.5	187.58	202.42	14.84	7.91
186.5	211.5	25	191.16	208.33	17.17	8.98
185	241	56	189.63	237.39	47.76	25.18
227	254	27	232.68	250.19	17.51	7.52
229	295	66	234.73	290.58	55.85	23.79
263	293.5	30.5	269.58	289.10	19.52	7.24
192	244.5	52.5	196.8	240.83	44.03	22.37
213	296.25	83.25	218.33	291.81	73.48	33.65
267	318	51	273.68	313.23	39.55	14.45
249	319	70	255.23	314.22	58.99	23.11
277	337	60	283.93	331.95	48.02	16.91
266	337.5	71.5	272.65	332.43	59.78	21.93
311.5	413.5	102	319.29	407.30	88.01	27.56
360	423	63	369	416.66	47.66	12.91
412	471	59	422.3	463.94	41.64	9.86
434	511	77	444.85	503.33	58.48	13.15
380	465	85	389.5	458.03	68.53	17.59
392	457	65	401.8	450.15	48.35	12.03
386	491	105	395.65	483.64	87.99	22.24
376	445	69	385.4	438.33	52.93	13.73
366	408	42	375.15	401.88	26.73	7.13
385.5	454	68.5	395.14	447.19	52.05	13.17
432	464	32	442.8	457.04	14.24	3.21
Averages		43.2			34.01	17.94

vast improvement over the annual gain of 12.67% made by the buy and hold investor.

The four situations we have examined so far are summarised in Table 1.8. Dividends have been omitted from each of the transactions in order to simplify the comparison.

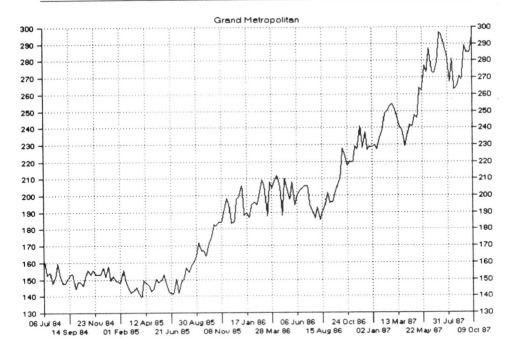

Figure 1.4 Very short term trends in the Grand Metropolitan share price between July 1984 and September 1987. These are represented by the share prices themselves

Two major points are illustrated by Table 1.8. The first of these is that as we take advantage of trends of shorter and shorter timescale, the gain made during the course of the trend falls lower and lower. This is a direct consequence of the properties of cyclical movements, and we shall see quite clearly later in this book that the longer the period of the cycle, the larger is the gain from the trough to the peak. Conversely, of course, very short term cycles make small gains. The second important point is that the *rate of gain*, expressed as an annual gain for comparison purposes, increases as we move from one very long term transaction of 18 years' duration to 13 transactions of lesser duration. As active investors it is this rate of gain that we have to maximise, since we will be continually ploughing gains back into subsequent investments. The rate of gain increases again as we move to transactions of a shorter timescale, averaging 12 weeks per transaction, but then only marginally improves as we move to even shorter time periods of 2.6 weeks. The reason for this is the effect of the dealing costs which really start to bite once we are down to lower gains per transaction. Thus there is a critical value of gain and a critical time period over which this gain is made below which there appears to be no advantage to the investor. This time period lies between 12 weeks' and 2.6 weeks' duration for Grand Metropolitan shares. For other shares, the

Table 1.6 Gains made in very short term trends in the Grand Metropolitan share price

Date	Price	Date	Price	Weeks	Rise	% rise	Factor
27 Jul 84	147	10 Aug 84	159	2	12	8.2	1.082
31 Aug 84	147	21 Sep 84	153	3	6	4.1	1.041
28 Sep 84	144	05 Oct 84	148	1	4	2.8	1.028
19 Oct 84	146	02 Nov 84	155	2	9	6.2	1.062
07 Dec 84	152.5	14 Dec 84	156.5	1	4	2.6	1.026
21 Dec 84	151	28 Dec 84	157.5	1	6.5	4.3	1.043
01 Feb 85	147.5	08 Feb 85	155	1	7.5	5.1	1.051
01 Mar 85	141.5	15 Mar 85	145	2	3.5	2.5	1.025
29 Mar 85	139	05 Apr 85	149	1	10	7.2	1.072
26 Apr 85	142.5	10 May 85	150	2	7.5	5.3	1.053
17 May 85	147.5	31 May 85	152.5	2	5	3.4	1.034
28 Jun 85	141	05 Jul 85	150	1	9	6.4	1.064
12 Jul 85	141.5	02 Aug 85	156.5	3	15	10.6	1.106
09 Aug 85	154	06 Sep 85	171.5	4	17.5	11.4	1.114
27 Sep 85	163.5	22 Nov 85	198	8	34.5	21.1	1.211
06 Dec 85	183	03 Jan 86	205.5	4	22.5	12.3	1.123
24 Jan 86	186.5	07 Feb 86	196	2	9.5	5.1	1.051
14 Feb 86	194	28 Feb 86	209	2	15	7.7	1.077
14 Mar 86	187.5	11 Apr 86	211.5	4	24	12.8	1.128
25 Apr 86	188	02 May 86	210	1	22	11.7	1.117
16 May 86	197.5	23 May 86	207.5	1	10	5.1	1.051
30 May 86	194	27 Jun 86	205.5	4	11.5	5.9	1.059
25 Jul 86	186	01 Aug 86	192.5	1	6.5	3.5	1.035
08 Aug 86	185	29 Aug 86	201.5	3	16.5	8.9	1.089
05 Sep 86	195.5	10 Oct 86	227.5	5	32	16.4	1.164
24 Oct 86	217.5	28 Nov 86	241	5	23.5	10.8	1.108
05 Dec 86	228	12 Dec 86	237.5	1	9.5	4.2	1.042
16 Jan 87	227	27 Feb 87	254	6	27	11.9	1.119
03 Apr 87	229	12 Jun 87	287	6	58	25.3	1.253
26 Jun 87	272.5	10 Jul 87	297	2	24.5	9.0	1.090
07 Aug 87	267.5	14 Aug 87	281	1	13.5	5.0	1.050
21 Aug 87	263	04 Sep 87	271	2	8	3.0	1.030
11 Sep 87	268.5	18 Sep 87	289	1	20.5	7.6	1.076
25 Sep 87	285	09 Oct 87	293.5	2	8.5	3.0	1.030
Averages				2.6	15.1	7.9	1.079

investor can determine this time period by going through the same exercise that we have in this chapter, but the results should be broadly comparable to those in Table 1.8.

COMPOUNDING SMALL GAINS INTO LARGE PROFITS

Now we move to the other important aspect of investment in shorter term trends compared with a buy and hold policy, and that is the question of the compounding effect on the gain of continually reinvesting the proceeds of

Table 1.7 Buying prices, selling prices and gains in very short term trends in the Grand Metropolitan share price adjusted for dealing costs

Buy price	Sell price	Gain	Real B.P.	Real S.P.	Real gain	% gain
147	159	12	150.68	156.62	5.94	3.94
147	153	6	150.68	150.71	0.03	0.02
144	148	4	147.6	145.78	−1.82	−1.23
146	155	9	149.65	152.68	3.03	2.02
152.5	156.5	4	156.32	154.16	−2.16	−1.38
151	157.5	6.5	154.78	155.14	0.36	0.23
147.5	155	7.5	151.19	152.68	1.49	0.98
141.5	145	3.5	145.04	142.82	−2.22	−1.53
139	149	10	142.48	146.77	4.29	3.01
142.5	150	7.5	146.06	147.75	1.69	1.16
147.5	152.5	5	151.19	150.22	−0.97	−0.64
141	150	9	144.53	147.75	3.22	2.23
141.5	156.5	15	145.04	154.16	9.12	6.28
154	171.5	17.5	157.85	168.93	11.08	7.02
163.5	198	34.5	167.6	195.03	27.43	16.38
183	205.5	22.5	187.58	202.42	14.84	7.91
186.5	196	9.5	191.17	193.06	1.89	0.99
194	209	15	198.85	205.87	7.02	3.53
187.5	211.5	24	192.19	208.33	16.14	8.40
188	210	22	192.7	206.85	14.15	7.34
197.5	207.5	10	202.44	204.39	1.95	0.96
194	205.5	11.5	198.85	202.42	3.57	1.79
186	192.5	6.5	190.65	189.62	−1.03	−0.54
185	201.5	16.5	189.63	198.48	8.85	4.67
195.5	227.5	32	200.39	224.09	23.7	11.83
217.5	241	23.5	222.94	237.39	14.45	6.48
228	237.5	9.5	233.7	233.94	0.24	0.10
227	254	27	232.68	250.19	17.51	7.53
229	287	58	234.73	282.7	47.97	20.44
272.5	297	24.5	279.32	292.55	13.23	4.74
267.5	281	13.5	274.19	276.79	2.60	0.95
263	271	8	269.58	266.94	−2.64	−0.98
268.5	289	20.5	275.22	284.67	9.45	3.43
285	293.5	8.5	292.13	289.1	−3.03	−1.04
Averages		15.1			7.39	3.7

Table 1.8 Length of trend, percentage gain and annual rate of gain for transactions in Grand Metropolitan shares

Transactions	Period (years)	Average length of trend (weeks)	% gain per trend	Equivalent annual gain
1	18	936	757	12.67
13	18	45	38.05	45.2
41	18	12	17.94	104.4
34	3.1	2.6	3.7	106.8

each transaction into the next one. We will see that this compounding effect will totally transform the profit levels we have been discussing so far into rates of gain that will turn modest amounts of starting capital into fortunes.

One way of illustrating the effect of compounding is to take the case of an investor who, like the rest of us, would like to double his money, starting with say £1000. To double this from just one buying and selling operation would require a 100% gain in the share price (for simplicity we assume no dealing costs). If he is relaxed about making more than one successive investment, reinvesting the proceeds from each one into the next in order to achieve his aim, then the gain he has to make from each investment is shown in Table 1.9 and Figure 1.5.

Table 1.9 The percentage gain per investment needed to double the original investment assuming proceeds are reinvested

Number of investments	1	2	3	4	5
% gain per investment	100	41.4	26.0	18.9	14.9
Number of investments	6	7	8	9	10
% gain per investment	12.2	10.4	9.1	8.0	7.2

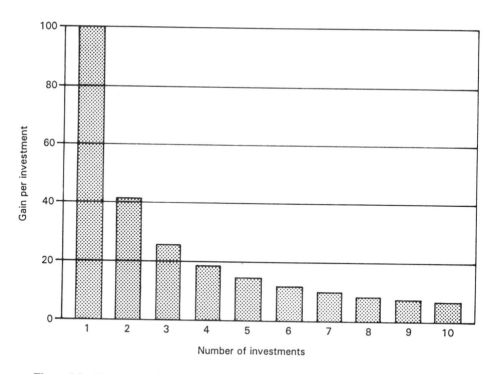

Figure 1.5 The percentage gain per investment required to double the starting capital for various numbers of consecutive investments

Thus with just two investments with which to double his money, he needs not 50% from each, but 41.4% from each, since the total proceeds of £1414 from his first investment are put into the second (he requires a 50% gain from each investment only if he intends to withdraw the gain each time, reinvesting only £1000 on each occasion). By the time he gets to five transactions over which to make the 100% gain, he needs to make only just under 15% from each of the five investments.

Taking the example of the gains made, after dealing costs, from the 13 upward trends in Grand Metropolitan, the compounding effect is best illustrated by expressing gains as factors rather than percentages. The cumulative data are shown in Table 1.10. The final column shows the increasing gain, expressed as a factor as each transaction is compounded. This gain is obtained by multiplying together all of the gain factors to that date. The net result is that after 13 such transactions, the starting capital has been multiplied by a factor of over 51! In percentage terms this gives a gain of 5000%. The advantage of this compounding effect has therefore turned what would have been a gain of 757% from buying and holding into almost seven times as much.

We can now begin to appreciate that although the gain per transaction starts to fall as we carry out more transactions within a time period such as 18 years, as was shown in Table 1.8, the magic of this compounding effect may well greatly outweigh this fall. To test this we can look at the situation where we carried out 41 transactions in the time period. Using the same method of multiplying together all of the gain factors, the final gain is a factor of 552, i.e. 55 100%.

Similarly, for the sequence of very short term transactions, the final gain obtained by multiplying together all of the 34 individual gain factors is 3.352, which in percentage terms is equal to 235% over the 3.1-year period.

Table 1.10 The cumulative gain obtained by reinvestment of proceeds of 13 successive transactions in Grand Metropolitan shares. Gains are adjusted for dealing costs

Buy price	Sell price	Real B.P.	Real S.P.	Real gain	% gain	Gain factor	Cumul. gain
44	70	45.1	68.95	23.85	52.9	1.529	1.529
67	102	68.68	100.47	31.79	46.29	1.4629	2.237
75.5	164	77.39	161.54	84.15	108.73	2.0873	4.669
153.5	174	157.3	171.39	14.09	8.96	1.0896	5.087
142.5	209	146.1	205.87	59.77	40.91	1.4091	7.168
194	272.5	198.85	268.4	69.55	34.97	1.3497	9.675
224.5	256.25	230.11	252.41	22.3	9.69	1.0969	10.613
228.5	317	234.21	312.25	78.04	33.32	1.3332	14.149
273.5	337	280.33	331.95	51.62	18.41	1.1841	16.753
266	510	272.65	502.35	229.7	84.25	1.8425	30.868
380	472	389.5	464.92	75.42	19.36	1.1936	36.844
408	491	418.2	483.64	65.44	15.64	1.1564	42.607
368	464	377.2	457.04	79.84	21.17	1.2117	51.627

Table 1.11 Length of trend, percentage gain, annual rate of gain and cumulative gain for transactions in Grand Metropolitan shares

Transactions	Period (years)	Average length of trend (weeks)	% gain per trend	Equivalent annual gain	Compound gain (%)
1	18	936	757	12.67	757
13	18	45	38.05	45.2	5062
41	18	12	17.94	104.4	55100
34	3.1	2.6	3.7	106.8	235

The overall compounded gains for the various transactions we have discussed in the chapter are shown in Table 1.11. We showed earlier that the equivalent annual gain for the transactions increased dramatically as we shortened the length of time for the transaction down to 12 weeks, but that it increased only marginally as we moved to transactions which lasted only 2.6 weeks. The same effect appears to carry through when we compound the gains by reinvestment into the succeeding transaction, since the final column where these values are displayed shows a fall-off from 55 100% for the 12-week transactions to 235% for the 2.6-week transactions. However, these two figures are not directly comparable, since the last one applies to a period of only 3.1 years, and not 18 years as do all the previous figures.

To bring the 3.352 gain factor over 3.1 years to one over 18 years we first bring it to an annual gain of 1.4772 by using the method we discussed at the beginning of this chapter. By raising this value to the power 18, we get the equivalent gain over 18 years, which is 1122. In percentage terms this is 112 100%.

Note that this theoretical gain of 112 100% has been obtained with our money working for us only part of the time. Taking Grand Metropolitan shares as an example, we can work out how much of the time we were invested by multiplying the average length of the particular trend, i.e. 45 weeks, 12 weeks and 2.6 weeks respectively, by the number of such trends that occurred over the 936-week period. Taking the 12-week trends as an example, there were 41 of these in the 936-week period. This means we were invested for 41 × 12 = 492 weeks out of the possible 936. During the rest of the time we would have been earning at the rate of what now appears to be the positively miserly 6% per annum or thereabouts that could have been obtained in the money market over this period since 1978. Quite obviously, therefore, we have to try to reach the position where our money is invested in rising shares 100% of the time, or as close to that as possible. If we can do that then we will obviously improve the gain made over an extended series of transactions enormously.

FROM THE THEORETICAL TO THE ACTUAL

So far in this chapter we have made two basic assumptions that we have not yet qualified: firstly, that we achieve perfect timing of our buying and selling operations, and secondly that none of the investments go wrong and lose us money. *We ignored this aspect simply to develop the argument that the gains which can be made from successive short term investment outweigh by tens, hundreds or even perhaps thousands of times the gain which is made by a simple buy and hold strategy.* These astronomical gains must therefore be considered to be theoretical in nature. **It will be totally impossible, whatever method we use, to buy in at the bottom and sell at the top of these trends consistently, year in and year out.** We might do it once or twice over the course of say a dozen transactions, but even that would be lucky. Furthermore, it is impossible to predict with 100% certainty that a trend will continue to rise so as to give us a guaranteed profit from every transaction. There will be occasions when random influences will cut short a trend, reversing its direction at such a speed that we cannot avoid a loss.

Being realistic, therefore, we have to downgrade our expectations for profit from the levels we have been using for the calculations in the previous tables. Firstly, we will make the assumption that the maximum gain per transaction after dealing costs will be 20%, i.e. using a round number slightly higher than the 17.94% which we showed previously would follow from perfect timing. Secondly, we will make the assumption that we are correct eight times out of ten, and for simplicity, when we are wrong, we will lose the same percentage that we make when we are correct. Thirdly, we will assume that the investor makes ten consecutive transactions, reinvesting the proceeds each time. Table 1.12 shows the resulting gains for such a series of investments where the gain (and loss), after dealing costs are taken into account, varies from 20% down to 1% per transaction.

These compounded gains run from 657%, i.e. multiplying our starting capital by 7.57 when we achieve a 20% gain per winning transaction and a 20% loss for losing transactions, down to 12.6% where we only achieve a 1% gain or loss.

To double our capital over these 20 transactions we need to reach the level of just over 6% per transaction. Note the improvement made for each additional 1% that can be squeezed out. Thus the investor reaching 7% per transaction will do 20% better overall than the investor reaching 6%.

Most of this book is dedicated towards improving the timing of buying and selling operations to such an extent that we should be able to capture gains of around 8 to 10% (after dealing costs) from each of those transactions which we have correctly forecast, while restricting our losses to similar levels from each of those transactions where the forecast goes wrong. From Table 1.12 it can be seen that this means that our capital will increase by a factor of two and a half to three times after 20 such transactions.

The remainder of this book is dedicated towards improving the performance of investors so that they can make these extra few percentage points out of each rise. Investors will be able to concentrate on the shorter term trends such as the 12-week trends we have been discussing for Grand Metropolitan. Techniques will be shown that enable the best shares to be

Table 1.12 Compounded gains made from 20 consecutive transactions for different gain levels per transaction. It is assumed that there are 16 winners and four losers. The loss for the losers is the same as the gain for the winners

Gain per transaction	Compounded gain factor	Compounded % gain
20	7.57	657
19	6.96	596
18	6.38	538
17	5.85	485
16	5.35	435
15	4.88	388
14	4.45	345
13	4.04	304
12	3.67	267
11	3.33	233
10	3.01	201
9	2.72	172
8	2.45	145
7	2.21	121
6	1.98	98
5	1.78	78
4	1.59	59
3	1.42	42
2	1.27	27
1	1.12	12

selected to take advantage of these short term trends. Techniques will also be shown that enable the investor to buy in very early in the life of the uptrend and sell not too far down from the end of the trend. It is suggested that investors develop a five-year horizon. In this time period, there will be between 20 and 25 transactions **in just one share** if trends of the order of 12 weeks are used. The investor who wishes to become more deeply involved can be invested simultaneously in a number of shares, subject to the restrictions mentioned in the final chapter.

In summary we can make the following points:

- Share prices consist of upward and downward trends of varying lengths of time.
- These trends fall into various categories, including those that last on average less than three weeks, those that last on average about 12 weeks and those that last on average just under one year.
- Average investors should make gains of about 10% out of trends which last on average for 12 weeks.
- By compounding such gains, average investors should be able to multiply their capital by about three over a series of 20 such transactions.
- Channel analysis will improve performance so that gains of many tens of times are possible over a long term if a full investment strategy is pursued as far as is practicable.

2

The Nature of Share Price Movement

INTRODUCTION

There has always been controversy over the way in which share prices move over the course of time, with chartists maintaining that prices can be predicted to a certain extent because historical patterns in the charts of share prices tend to recur from time to time. These methods of analysis rest heavily on the recognition of the start of a pattern formation so that the subsequent movement can be anticipated. On the other hand, the fundamentalists believe that the key to investment success lies in such factors as the way in which a company is managed, the quality and appeal of its products, and the strength or weakness of its balance sheet.

They believe for the most part that chartist techniques are just mumbo-jumbo and that the past history of share price plays no part in the future movement. If pressed about the nature of share price movement, many fundamentalists would state that they believe that share prices move on a random basis and therefore cannot be predicted. In doing this, they ignore the obvious corollary: if prices move randomly, there is no advantage in studying the fundamentals of any company since the random share price will bear no relationship to these fundamentals.

While fundamentalists are for the most part hostile to chartists, the reverse is not true. Chartists will agree that there should be some relationship between the way in which a company is run and its future share price. Certainly it would be unreasonable to expect that a company that is continually making losses will show a strong share price. Chartists are of the opinion that all the positive aspects of a company's performance are reflected in the share price, and therefore an analyst can take a shortcut by looking at the share price and not the fundamentals. This author stands with the chartists on this point about the relationship between the share price and the fundamentals, believing that what moves a share price upwards is not the quality of the management or the products or the balance sheet, but investors' views about the company's potential. Some investors' views may indeed be influenced strongly by the fact that they have carried out an analysis of the company's balance sheet or market strengths. Other investors may simply have read comments in the press. Yet others may have applied some technical analysis of the share price chart and come to a conclusion about the future movement of the share price. It is the sum total of these different views, many of which will be contradictory, that will add up to the pressure in the market place that will cause the share price to move. When all views are the same, the price will move rapidly, while if they are nearly in balance, the price will drift more or less sideways. Grafted on to all of this will be the views of the market makers, since they have to balance their books also. There will be some shares which attract no comment and attract no technical analysis because they have generated no excitement in the past. In such cases, therefore, it is unreasonable, however strong the fundamentals are, to expect the share price to move upwards.

This author takes the position that everything an investor needs to know about a company is stated in its share price movement. *It will be simpler and quicker for an investor to discover how to analyse share price movement than to study the company itself, and the result of this price analysis will tell the investor the most important fact: how other investors feel about that company.*

Where this author does not stand with the chartists is in their simplistic approach to share price analysis. In its most trivial form chartism depends upon sets of rules which have to be followed without any other understanding. Thus the chartists will make statements such as "buy when the share price moves above the x-day moving average", where x depends upon the chartist you are speaking to, or "sell when the ten-day average falls below the twenty-day average". Such a set of blind rules should play no part in the thinking man's investment armamentarium. The human race has always striven to understand the reasons for the behaviour of the physical world, and share price movement should be no exception. A Pavlovian response to a set of circumstances will ultimately lead to disaster, since the stock market is always ready with the unexpected. Experienced chartists can probably correctly predict whether a share price will move up or down about 55% of the time, but this means they are wrong about 45% of the time. The dangers of a set of rules which work only just over half of the time are obvious. Investor psychology is such that the investor is always trying to avoid selling a holding in the belief that an adverse movement is only a minor aberration in the expected upward trend, and will surely correct itself before too long. Nearly all investors have seen a good paper profit from a good buying decision evaporate because of this reluctance to sell. If we are going to work to any set of rules, the reasoning behind them must be perfectly clear, so that those occasions when the share price does not seem to be following the rules can be understood for what they are—times when we have to be more flexible about our interpretation of the rules.

By this more logical approach of trying to understand why share prices move as they do, we should be able to improve our predictive techniques so that we can almost always recognise the start of a new upward or downward trend. We will be able to recognise when we have made a mistake about the start of a new upward trend, and be able to act quickly to close the losing position before the loss is anything other than a trivial one. We will be able to follow the old stock market rule: "let your profits run and cut your losses". This will be a great advance for most investors, who seem to do exactly the opposite, selling the share when there is still plenty of profit to come, but staying with a share which is falling rapidly, because they are convinced that it will soon change direction.

ARE SHARE PRICES RANDOM?

The simple response to this question would be to point out that the world's stock exchanges depend upon prices not being random. If they were random, then one might as well pick shares for investment with a pin, or forgo the stock market altogether and leave one's money in the money market, earning the best rate of interest available. The vast array of stock market analysts employed by various institutions would be totally superfluous and investment writers like myself would have to turn to other activities.

The existence of investment commentators, besides indicating that the movement of share prices may not be random, also raises an interesting philosophical point. Their existence may be the reason that share prices are not random, in the sense that their comments in newspapers may distort what would otherwise be a random process. Just suppose, for example, that Guinness shares were moving in a random fashion until one day the investment columns of two or three newspapers suggested that Guinness shares represented a good buy. Many of their readership will take their advice and start buying these shares. The inevitable logic of supply and demand dictates that the price of Guinness shares will then start to rise. If these same newspapers continue to push Guinness shares as a good buy, then more and more readers will begin to take notice, and the share price will continue to rise. The rise will not continue forever, but at some point will reverse itself. This is because an increasing number of these new holders of Guinness shares will decide that they have now made sufficient profit to have satisfied their objectives, or will decide that all good things must come to an end, and will now act in a contrary way to the advice being offered and will sell their shares. This selling pressure will increase, thereby causing the Guinness share price to fall. Eventually we can conclude that the Guinness share price has reverted back to its original random movement.

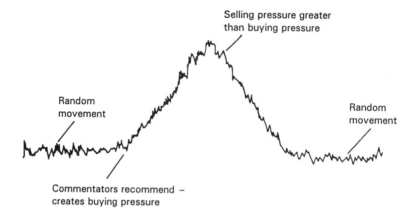

Selling pressure greater
than buying pressure

Random
movement

Random
movement

Commentators recommend –
creates buying pressure

Figure 2.1 Random price movement becoming non-random for a period of time due to favourable press comment

This example serves to show quite clearly that even if we accept the premise that some or most of the time a share price is behaving randomly, then there will be occasions when because of press comment the price will move in a non-random manner. This can be illustrated by the type of movement shown in Figure 2.1.

Just to restate the position so far: we assumed that the Guinness share price was moving randomly until a random event (comments in newspapers) caused the price to move in a non-random fashion for a period of time. The non-random movement was caused by a bandwagon effect of investors reading and acting on comment in their newspapers.

A closer inspection of Figure 2.1 shows that the day-to-day fluctuations, when viewed in isolation, are still apparent even when the underlying long term trend is rising.

Since we can accept that a random event such as a newspaper article was the trigger to an upward and then a downward price movement, it is but a short step to an improved model of share price movement:

1. Share prices contain random day-to-day movement.
2. Share prices contain upward and downward trends.
3. The start and end of a particular trend is a random event.

By the word "trend" we mean an underlying price movement that lasts for more than a few days, and may last as long as many years.

To determine that prices are or are not random is difficult, and would take us into a realm of mathematics that would be out of place in a book of this nature. However, we can make some progress by taking a simpler approach. To do this it is necessary to take a close look at daily price changes in a share such as Guinness. In Figure 2.2 are plotted the daily changes in closing price, over a 1000-day period up to September 1996.

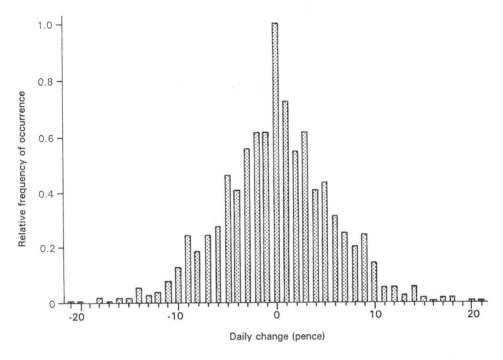

Figure 2.2   The daily price changes in Guinness over a 1000-day period are plotted as relative frequency of occurrence of a change versus that change

The plot shows the relative frequency of occurrence of various price changes, with the most frequent change being zero, i.e. the price on one day is the same as that on the previous day. For comparison with Figure 2.3, the most frequent occurrence is given a frequency of 1. The largest changes shown in the figure are a rise of 21p and a fall of 21p. The important feature of Figure 2.2 is its shape, rather than specific values.

If daily price changes in Guinness over the period of time in question were totally random, then the shape of the curve in Figure 2.2 would be identical with that shown in Figure 2.3, the classical probability shape. It can be seen that the general shape of Figure 2.2 approximates to the probability shape, with the main distortion being that the central value, corresponding to zero daily change, is too large. If this value is reduced, then the shape gets closer to the ideal, with most frequencies not too far away from the value predicted for total randomness. Thus a simple deduction from the shape of the curve in Figure 2.2 is that there is a great deal of random behaviour in the daily change in the Guinness share price, and that the major departure from total random behaviour lies in the greater than expected incidence of no-change days. Thus we can say that random and non-random daily behaviour are co-existing.

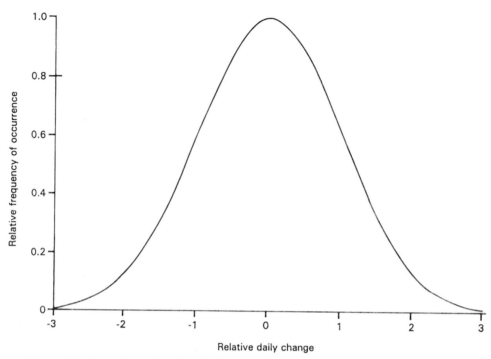

Figure 2.3   A totally random distribution of daily price changes would have the shape of the above curve

A moment's thought would lead us to the proper conclusion that since there is an indeterminate amount of random behaviour in daily price movements, and that the majority of daily movements lie within the range of plus or minus 10p (Figure 2.2), there is no profit to be made in an investment made solely on the basis of a prediction of the price movement on a particular day. We need to move from daily movements to longer term trends where the price movement is much larger.

The first, inescapable conclusion is that since daily movements exhibit a high degree of randomness, then price trends over a succession of days built up from these individual movements must also show a high degree of randomness. This can be addressed in an unusual way.

In Figure 2.4 we show the chart of the Guinness share price covering the period since 1983. The data are weekly in this case in order to present a long price history. It can be seen that a long term uptrend was sustained from September 1988 to mid-1992, before the price retreated somewhat and then stayed within a trading range.

Except for the fact that the timescale is very much longer, the chart resembles Figure 2.1, where we took the example of a random movement that then became transformed into a non-random movement by press comment. In Figure 2.4 we appear to have a random price movement

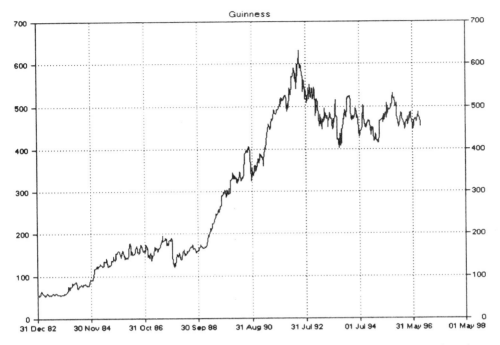

Figure 2.4 The price movement in Guinness shares since 1983. The data are plotted weekly

occurring, which then develops quite obviously into a non-random movement for reasons which are not obvious. Unlike Figure 2.1, the price has not yet returned to its levels at the beginning of the chart period.

It is interesting to see what a randomly created share price looks like when plotted. This is done by taking a starting value, such as 200p, and then randomly setting a value for the change over the following week. The change is added or subtracted from the previous day's calculated closing price. Such a chart is shown in Figure 2.5. The price is random in the sense that it can move upwards or downwards from the previous value, but we have put a 10% limit on the movement in either direction. This is done to come as close as possible to real life, since we know by experience that prices do not move in huge jumps from day to day. The purists might argue that in doing this we have moved away from a completely random model, but this is not a significant restriction in terms of what we are trying to achieve.

There are many similarities between the random movement in Figure 2.5 and the movement of the Guinness share price in Figure 2.4 in the sense that underlying trends can be observed with random variations superimposed upon them. It could be argued that the only thing that really distinguishes the two types of chart is the much stronger upward trend observed in the Guinness share price, but that in general the chart could

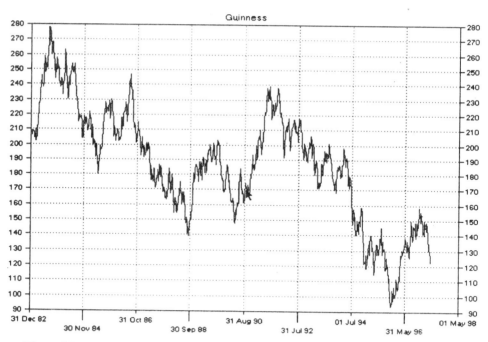

Figure 2.5 A reconstructed chart of Guinness shares made by randomly calculating the change from the previous week. The starting value is 200p

be that of any share. Chartists could draw trendlines and the like on this random chart just as on any other chart of a share price. While the similarities to share charts would lead to the conclusion that share price movement is totally random, simply looking at the chart in Figure 2.5 is not a rigorous mathematical test of random behaviour.

Fortunately for us, the model of share price movement that we put forward earlier in this chapter is a better reflection of how share prices move than is a model in which we take all price movement to be totally random. Even so, our model is not perfect, being only partly true. It is true that share prices contain random day-to-day and week-to-week movement, but what is not true is the statement that the start and end of a price trend is itself a random event. Share prices are essentially driven by these trends, but the beginning and end of a trend is not a totally random event. It is this fact that makes the methods used in this book workable, since if day-to-day price movement is random and the start and end of the trends are random, then the share price is totally unpredictable.

Without getting into the realms of probability theory, it is possible to demonstrate that while individual daily or weekly price changes can be accepted as having a great deal of random content, trends are much less random. For this purpose we can define a trend as being a succession of upward movements or downward movements on a daily or weekly basis.

The procedure is to take the Guinness share weekly price movements since 1983 and note all of the weekly changes. These are put into a pool. The same starting price of 54.5p on 7th January 1983, is used. The change over the following week is determined by randomly selecting from all of the changes which have now been put into the pool. From this change the following week's price can of course be determined. The following week another change is taken from the pool. The procedure is repeated until a reconstructed price has been obtained for Guinness over the same period as the real price change occurred. Thus we have used the actual price changes which occurred in Guinness, but randomly changed the order in which they occurred. The result of this is shown in the chart in Figure 2.6. As with the previous random chart, there is nothing unusual about it, and it could be the chart of a real share price.

Since the chart has been reconstructed by randomly selecting price changes from the pool, then by using a computer, this process can be repeated as many times as required, with the result being different in each case.

The usefulness of this experiment lies not in the appearance of the charts themselves, but in a calculation of the number of times the price changes direction over the timescale used. In virtually every case, there are

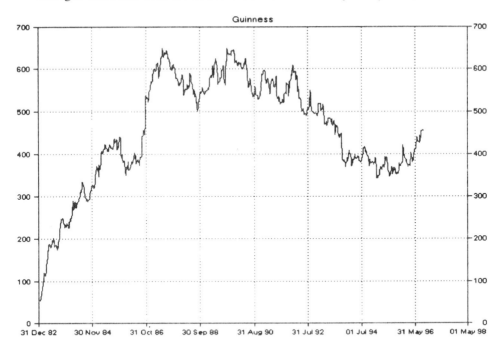

Figure 2.6   The reconstructed weekly price movement in Guinness shares since 1983. From the same starting value of 54.5p, the order of weekly price changes has been randomly changed

considerably more changes of direction in the reconstructed prices than in the real ones. Since there are fewer changes of direction in real prices, the sequences of upward or downward price movements must last longer. Thus there are more upward or downward trends in real prices, i.e. trends are more persistent in the real prices. Since the reconstructed prices have been generated by a totally random selection from the pool, this means that trends are subject to less random behaviour in share prices than would be predicted on the basis that the daily or weekly changes which go to make up the trends have a high random content. It is this increased persistence of trends that will enable us to make profits out of investment in shares.

Because of this increased persistence in the trends, and because of the fact that daily and weekly price movements, although having a high random content, do not have a 100% random content, then probably 70% of share price movement is not random, and is therefore predictable if the correct techniques are applied. The analysis of cycles in share price data, discussed in Chapter 6, also confirms this as a ball-park figure for non-random behaviour.

The technique of channel analysis, especially when used in conjunction with moving averages of various types, is able to extract most of this predictable movement from the share price data, thus giving the investor the most powerful prediction technique currently available.

We can predict the start and end of these price trends with a fair measure of success by adopting a realistic approach of developing "prediction boxes". This means we do not say "the price will be 285p on 17th November 1997". We do say "the price will enter the prediction area at the beginning of November where the downward trend will have an increasing probability of reversing direction, with the lowest price being in the range of 280p to 290p". The difference between these two statements is the fact that in the first case we would be totally positive about a situation that it is impossible to be positive about, whereas in the second case we are taking into account the partially random nature of trends. Another important point is that the further into the future we try to predict, the greater will be the error involved in this prediction. The fact of the matter is that we do not need to know approximate price movements more than about three months ahead. This will be perfectly adequate for making substantial profits, as was discussed in the last chapter.

It is interesting to see how seriously some sections of the press take the idea of long term prediction of share prices by some of the gurus of the industry. Just prior to the start of each new year the business sections of the quality newspapers always poll a number of analysts for their predictions of where the FTSE100 Index will be at the end of the year. Be assured, this is not done as a little bit of Christmas fun, since both the columnist and the guru being polled seriously believe that this is a worthwhile exercise. They are saying between them that they know exactly what you out there will be doing on the investment scene in a year's time! Just keep cuttings of these predictions and have your own bit of fun reading them in the future.

At some points in share price histories different trends will be featured particularly strongly, while at other times the price just seems to meander along with no apparent direction. Quite obviously, shares that move in the latter fashion will be useless to us as investors, since we will not be able to predict any future price movement. On the other hand, shares where the trends are readily observable offer the possibility of using predictive techniques in order to determine the best buying and selling times for those shares. Since there are so many shares quoted on the stock market, there will be no shortage of shares which fall into this category. We will show in this book that such is the diversity of shares that it will be possible to remain virtually fully invested, since when the time comes to sell one share, another will present itself as a good buying opportunity. It will not even be necessary to keep track of large numbers of shares. The 100 shares which comprise the FTSE100 Index, plus the shares which form the mid-250 Index, will provide plenty of opportunity. A further advantage to the investor in staying with these 350 shares is that the spread of prices, i.e. the difference between the buying and selling price of a share at a particular point in time, is much less than is the case with the shares of companies which have smaller capitalisations.

3

Trends in Share Prices

In the last chapter we arrived at the conclusion that prices consist of random day-to-day movement plus trends which by definition were non-random. We also came to the conclusion that the beginning and end of trends were random. In this chapter we will examine the concept of trends much more clearly, and show that the beginning and end of trends are not quite as random as we first thought.

What do we mean by a trend in share prices? A trend is a movement that lasts for a certain period of time. What makes trends difficult to visualise in share prices is that upon any trend can be superimposed many other trends of differing time periods. The object of this book is to look at methods of isolating particular trends and develop a better method of doing this. Once we have isolated a trend we can then make use of it for investment purposes, buying a share that is just entering an uptrend, and selling that share when it enters a downtrend. We will find that trends of very short time periods will be of little use to us, since the price movement they cause will be too little to cover even the costs of the buying and selling transactions, let alone make any considerable profit. On the other hand, trends of very long periods, say many years, will already be under way when we wish to invest in the market, and we will probably not wish to wait until they change to a favourable direction. We therefore will have to accept these, if they are moving downwards, as a negative influence on our profit potential. Because of this aspect we will have to base our investment decisions mainly on trends of medium timescale, say from about five weeks' up to one or two years' duration.

Since all of these trends are mixed up together, it is easier to start the discussion by looking at the shortest possible trend, and working outwards from that point.

If we take the completely open view that we have no idea whether the trend is a straight line or a curve, then this will give us a starting point for the shortest possible trend. A straight line requires only two points to define it, whereas the simplest curve—a circle—requires at least three points to define it. Since we have decided that the trend may be a curve, then the minimum number of share prices which will define a trend will be three. The finest detail which it is sensible to work on will be daily share prices, but for those investors who have so far used weekly prices, the same conclusions about trends will be drawn. The only difference is that weekly prices can only define weekly trends, while daily prices can define daily trends. Thus daily prices will highlight trends of shorter timespan than three weeks (three weekly points are the minimum to define a weekly trend). The availability of daily prices will also be an advantage for highlighting trends which may not be a whole number of weeks, e.g. a trend of five and a half weeks. In this book we will analyse both daily and weekly prices.

THE SHORTEST POSSIBLE TREND

The shortest possible trend, as we have seen, is based on three share prices. Although in a sense we could say that a sideways movement in prices is not a trend, and that the chances of a trend being exactly sideways are not high, it is best for this discussion to categorise trends as being sideways, upwards or downwards.

As a starting point we can consider that there is no random aspect to this three-point trend and that the trend is a linear one. The three possible trend directions are then shown in Figure 3.1. A, B and C are the three consecutive price values, and they fall exactly on the trend lines which are drawn as dashed lines.

These three points which lie on a straight line may be the first three points of a trend which continues for tens or maybe hundreds of points, all lying on the same straight line. In such cases the trend can be considered to be a medium or long term trend. However, the heading for this section is "The Shortest Possible Trend". Implicit in this heading is the fact that after three points, the trend has come to an end. It can come to an end by entering a region where the price just moves totally randomly on a day-to-

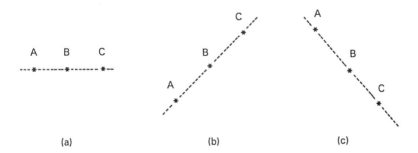

Figure 3.1 Three-point linear trends: (a) sideways trend, A = B = C; (b) uptrend, C > B > A; (c) downtrend, C < B < A

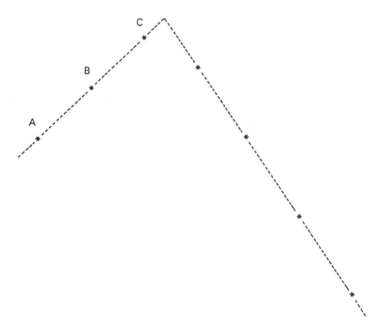

Figure 3.2   The transformation of a three-point uptrend into a new downtrend

day basis or it can come to an end by becoming a new trend moving in a different direction and at a different slope from the original. We can only determine this fact by having more prices than these three upon which to base the analysis. The completion of one trend and the transformation into a new trend is illustrated by the example in Figure 3.2.

Later in this book we will take a differing view from that taken by chartists, who consider most trends as being straight lines. We will take the view that trends are curved, and that those occasions where they appear to be straight lines are the special cases where the radius of the curve is so large that it is virtually a straight line. In mathematics a straight line is a curve of infinite radius, but in share price analysis we can consider that a straight line trend is one which is based on cycles of tens of years of duration.

If we now move to curved three-point trends, we have the picture shown in Figure 3.3. The sideways trend puts us in some difficulty, since the sideways movement has to be a straight line. We cannot therefore have a curved sideways trend of only three-point duration, but only uptrends and downtrends.

The end of a linear trend was fairly easy to envisage, since the straight line simply changed direction or moved into a random area of movement as we showed by the examples in Figure 3.2. Curved trends based on circular curves have another dimension to them, and that is the radius of

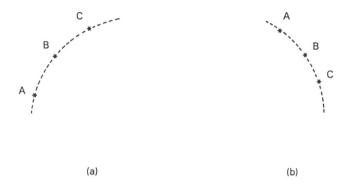

(a)   (b)

Figure 3.3   Curved three-point trendlines: (a) uptrend; (b) downtrend

curvature of the circle. The important fact here is that if we know the radius of the circle, we know when the trend will change direction from being an uptrend to a downtrend, and vice versa. We stated earlier that a circle is defined by only three points. If our uptrends are segments of a circle we can see how the highest points can be predicted by the two cases shown in Figure 3.4. Similarly, if our downtrends are segments of a circle, we can see how the lowest points can be predicted by the two cases shown in Figure 3.5.

Since the circles of smallest radius are those where the trend peaks out or bottoms out much sooner than in the case where the circles have a large

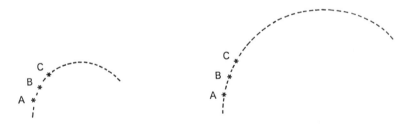

Figure 3.4   Curved uptrends of different radius

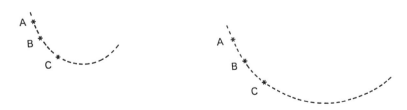

Figure 3.5   Curved downtrends of different radius

radius, this leads to the important fact that short term trends are based on curves of small radius, while long term trends are based on curves of large radius. If a trend is a segment of a circle, and if we can determine the radius of that segment, then we can predict future prices that lie on that trend.

TRENDS ARE CYCLICAL

It has been useful to consider trends as segments of circles in order to develop the discussion clearly. Now we can move to the major theme of this book, which is that trends are cyclical in nature, i.e. that they have peaks and troughs which recur at intervals. True cycles have peaks and troughs that recur at fixed intervals, but we shall see that cycles in the share prices suffer from the application of the old saying that nothing is certain in the stock market. Cycles in the stock market suffer from a random variation so that not only is there some uncertainty as to when the next peak or trough in a particular cycle will occur, but there is also uncertainty as to the importance of the next peak, so that it might make virtually no contribution to the share price itself.

Cycles in stock market prices are sine waves, and it is necessary to spend some time discussing the properties of sine waves at a fairly superficial level in order to gain more understanding about how we can use the properties of sine waves to predict future share price movement.

Properties of Sine Waves

A sine wave such as that shown in Figure 3.6 is completely described if we know three quantities. These are:

• Wavelength or frequency
• Amplitude
• Phase

As shown in the figure, the wavelength is the distance between one peak and the next peak, or one trough and the next trough. The units in which the wavelength is measured depend on the field of study, thus radio waves are measured in metres. For the stock market, we are concerned with daily or weekly price movements, and therefore our wavelengths will be measured in days or weeks, or for long term movements, years. Although we will not be using frequency as a measurement, it is defined as the inverse of the wavelength, so for a cycle in a share price which has a wavelength of 13 weeks, i.e. 0.25 years, there would be 1/0.25 = 4 cycles per year. The frequency is therefore 4 per year.

The amplitude is the vertical distance from trough to peak, and in the case of stock market cycles this will be measured in a unit of currency such

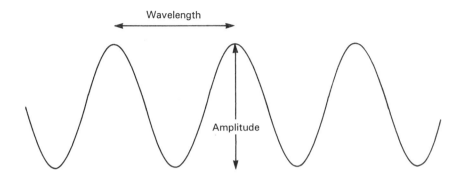

Figure 3.6   A sine wave showing the meaning of amplitude and wavelength

as pence, or for an index such as the Financial Times Index in points. Both wavelength and amplitude are illustrated in Figure 3.6.

The phase of a sine wave is a slightly more difficult concept, but it represents how far along from some arbitrary starting point the sine wave is. It is best illustrated by showing two sine waves, which are identical in amplitude and wavelength, that are in phase, and the same two sine waves when they are out of phase, as shown in Figure 3.7. When two sine waves are in phase, their peaks and troughs occur at exactly the same point in time.

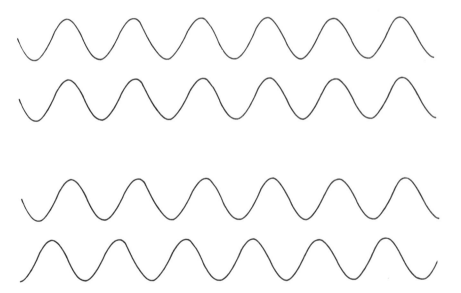

Figure 3.7   Upper: two sine waves exactly in phase; lower: two sine waves out of phase

For the mathematically minded, the equation for a sine wave of relevance to the stock market is:

$$\text{price at time } t = \text{amplitude} \times \sin(F + Wt)$$

where

$W = 2 \times \pi/N$

N is the wavelength in days, weeks or years

$\pi = 3.142$

t is a time in the same units as N, i.e. days, weeks or years

F is a measurement of phase and is simply the number of days, weeks or years along the sine wave from the zero point where the wave is on a rising trend. Note that all the time units must be the same.

For a cycle of any wavelength, this equation will enable us to calculate the share price at any time.

Before we move on, we have to correlate the trends we discussed in Chapter 1 with these sine waves. We talked in Chapter 1 about uptrends where the average trend lasted for say 12 weeks or 48.8 weeks. Now an uptrend is simply one half of a sine wave, since the other half will be a downtrend. Therefore the 12-week trends are derived from cycles which have an average wavelength of 24 weeks, and the 48.8-week trends are derived from cycles which have an average wavelength of just under two years.

The Real World

So far we have come to the conclusion that share prices contain random movement and underlying trends, and that the basic form of an underlying trend is a cyclical wave. In the real world, a share price chart consists of a complex mixture of random movements and cyclical trends of differing wavelengths from a few days up to tens of years from peak to peak. We have already defined what we mean by the amplitude of such waves, and we shortly show that the amplitude of waves of long wavelength is greater than that of waves of shorter wavelength. A four-year cycle will cause the share price to rise from trough to peak in two years, and this rise from trough to peak will be several times as large as that caused by, say, a four-week cycle in the share price.

The Effect of Random Movement on a Trend

Since share price movement is composed of a number of trends plus a random price movement, it is best to start from the simplest case and show the effect of adding some random price movement to just one cycle. This is

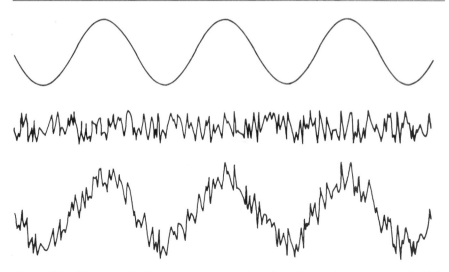

Figure 3.8 How a cyclical trend (upper trace) and random price movement (middle trace) combine to give the final observed price movement (lower trace)

shown in Figure 3.8. The final result is close in appearance to parts of almost any chart of stock market share prices.

The process of adding together the random data and the trend is exactly what it says—we take two sets of values and add them together to get the final result. To illustrate this point, the actual data for the random movement and the cyclic trend are given in Table 3.1. By adding corresponding values together we get the final result, which when plotted gives the combined trace shown in the lower part of Figure 3.8.

The data for the random movement and the trend were calculated by using a computer. If you wish to try the same exercise of adding together various sets of random data and cyclic trends you can calculate values for the cyclic trend by using the equation for a sine wave given previously. If you do not have a computer you can use a scientific calculator to work out the sine values for you, or you can use a graphical method. Just draw the smoothest approximation to a sine wave that you can on a sheet of graph paper and read off the vertical values from the graph at constant intervals across the paper, say every centimetre or every two millimetres. Draw a portion of random price movement and read off those values at the same intervals across the page. The two sets of values can be added and replotted to give the final result.

Adding Cyclical Trends Together

The above exercise of adding together a random movement to just one cyclical trend is relatively simple, and as we saw in Figure 3.8 gives a result which is very similar to some portions of real share price charts. It is also

Table 3.1 How a cyclical trend and random movement are additive. The values if plotted will give one section of the traces in Figure 3.8

Week	Cyclic value	Random value	Sum
1	0.35	13.42	13.77
2	1.87	14.95	16.82
3	4.55	14.80	19.35
4	8.27	13.33	21.60
5	12.88	0.07	12.95
6	18.19	6.68	24.87
7	23.90	3.13	27.03
8	30.02	14.72	44.74
9	36.06	10.85	46.91
10	41.85	8.51	50.36
11	47.16	1.11	48.27
12	51.76	15.36	67.12
13	55.47	10.27	65.74
14	58.14	11.28	69.42
15	59.66	14.82	74.48
16	59.03	4.62	63.65
17	56.92	9.28	66.20
18	53.70	2.57	56.27
19	49.51	9.69	59.20
20	44.52	1.11	45.63
21	38.94	7.25	46.19
22	33.00	11.42	44.42
23	26.92	19.80	46.72
24	20.98	5.80	26.78
25	15.40	13.15	28.55
26	10.42	18.78	29.20
27	6.25	7.60	13.85
28	3.04	17.81	20.85
29	0.95	15.96	16.91

fairly easy to add together two different cycles, i.e. of two different wavelengths, since once again we just add together the numerical values of each cycle at the same points in time and replot the result. As a start we can add together two cycles, one of which has twice the wavelength and twice the amplitude of the other. Where the difficulty comes in is in deciding on the phase of the cycles, i.e. how far along each cycle we are when we start the addition process. If we start with the two cycles exactly in phase, e.g. we start each one halfway up the rising portion, we get the picture shown in Figure 3.9, i.e. both cycles are rising at the start of the exercise and therefore the cycles are additive for this first part of the trace. If we carry out the process with one cycle out of phase with the other, we get a different result which will depend on how far out of phase the two cycles are. In Figure 3.10 we start the upper cycle in the same position as before, but the lower cycle, instead of starting halfway up the rising side, starts halfway

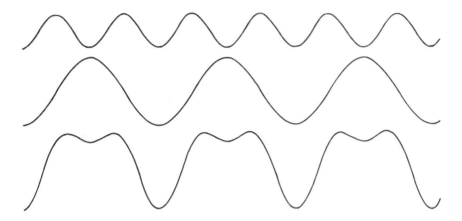

Figure 3.9 The addition of two cycles, one having twice the wavelength and amplitude of the other. The starting points are in phase

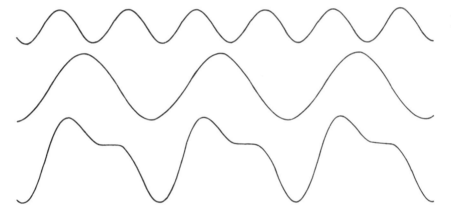

Figure 3.10 The addition of the two cycles from Figure 3.9 where the starting points are out of phase

down the falling side. This means that at the start of the exercise one cycle is rising and one cycle is falling and so the cycles are subtractive for this first part of the trace.

One point that is not obvious is that if we look at a long enough time period, encompassing enough peaks and troughs, we pass through all possible combinations of the two cycles provided that cycles are not related to each other by powers of two. In the latter case the relationship between the cycles remains constant. In all other cases one cycle will catch up and overtake the other so that all combinations eventually occur. Thus patterns similar to those in Figures 3.9 and 3.10 will be present within the same trace, and will recur at intervals. This is an important point that will be discussed soon when we consider chart patterns and how they

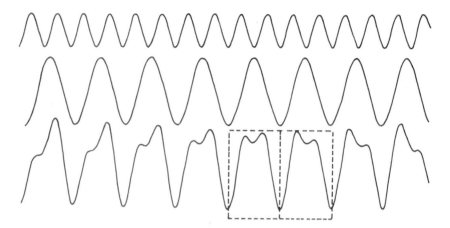

Figure 3.11 How patterns reappear in combinations of cycles irrespective of their starting points if a long enough timescale is taken, provided the cycles are not related to each other by powers of two. The dotted rectangles show patterns similar to those that were displayed in Figures 3.9 and 3.10

sometimes fail, but it can be illustrated quite readily by starting off the combination of the two cycles we used in Figures 3.9 and 3.10 in yet another relationship, where they are both on a rising trend at the start of the traces. The result of adding these two cycles for a longer time period is shown in Figure 3.11. We can see readily that both of the patterns we saw in Figures 3.9 and 3.10 occur at different points in this longer time period.

Figures 3.9 and 3.10 can be used to illustrate a very useful point besides the obvious one that the result of adding the two cycles depends on where they stand relatively to each other. This is that the cycle of longer wavelength, which also has the larger amplitude, is the cycle that dominates the share price movement and is the one which we can call the major cycle. The cycle of shorter wavelength and lesser amplitude, which we can call the minor cycle, causes fluctuations in this major underlying trend. Note that where the trough of the minor cycle corresponds to the trough of the major cycle the price is carried lower than on any other occasion, and conversely, where the peak of the minor cycle coincides with the peak of the major cycle the price is carried higher than on any other occasion. Note also that the rate of rise from such very low points is very high, and their equivalent in share price movements, i.e. points where several cycles each reach a low point simultaneously, offer outstanding profit potential.

CHART PATTERNS AND CYCLES

Chartists rely on the identification of various chart patterns in order to be able to predict the future movement of share prices, on the basis that a pattern behaved in a certain way in the past and therefore should continue to do so in the future. Thus the important aspect to a chartist is the development of a formation that can be recognised as the start of one of these patterns. We mentioned in an earlier chapter that expert chartists are right about 55% of the time and wrong about 45% of the time. The reason is their failure to understand why such chart patterns are formed. If they could understand why such patterns exist then they would also understand why such patterns do not always develop the way that the chartist thinks they will, in other words why they sometimes fail, causing losses where there should have been profits.

Chief amongst the patterns dear to the chartists we can find support lines, resistance lines, uptrend lines, downtrend lines, double tops and double bottoms, head and shoulders and inverse head and shoulders. We will show that all of these patterns can be explained quite simply by the combination of numbers of cycles of different wavelengths and amplitudes. A particular pattern appears because these cycles have at that particular time the correct relationship of their phases. As we pointed out above, the particular relationship between phases recurs at constant intervals in time, although for complex combinations of cycles this may well happen many years apart. The fact that certain formations fail to complete the expected total pattern is easily explained on the basis that not all the cycles are in the correct relationship at the start of the pattern.

This reason for the failure of patterns can be developed slightly further. We stated in the last section that the major component, i.e. the component of longest wavelength and amplitude, was the dominant one, and the minor component added some finer detail to this dominant movement. The gross appearance of a pattern in the chart depends upon the major component, but the formation will not develop to the expected pattern if some of the minor components are moving contrariwise to the way they moved when the pattern was formed in the previous history of the share price or if they are shifted slightly in their phases.

The following figures show how the combination of different cycles at certain points in time can lead to recognisable patterns and the circumstances under which the pattern can fail.

1. Support and Resistance Lines (Figure 3.12(a) and (b))

These are formed by the combination of very short term cycles and a very long term cycle which is at its trough or peak. Very long term cycles of say eight years' wavelength appear to be horizontal for a considerable period at their peaks and troughs. The price finally bounces back up from a support line or down from a resistance line, or penetrates the support/ resistance line, because of the intervention of an intermediate term cycle. If this is just sweeping up from its trough, it will take the share price with it, which means a bounce back up from a support line (the pattern continues)

(a)   (b)

Figure 3.12   (a) Support line; (b) resistance line

or a penetration up through a resistance line (pattern ends, but a good buying signal). On the other hand, if the intermediate cycle is just bending down from its peak, it will carry the share price down, which means a bounce back from a resistance line (pattern continues) or a penetration of a resistance line (pattern ends, take as a selling signal).

2. Uptrend and Downtrend (Figure 3.13(a) and (b))

These two cases are formed for the same reasons as the above support/ resistance lines from a combination of very short term cycles and a long term cycle which is not at its peak or trough as above, but in an uptrend or downtrend. Again, very long term cycles of more than say eight years' wavelength will have rising and falling sides that appear as almost straight lines for a period of time. The price breaks away from these by the inter-vention of an intermediate term cycle. If the latter is just passing its trough it will cause the share price to surge upwards. For an uptrend, therefore, the effect is to cause the uptrend to steepen sharply, while for a downtrend

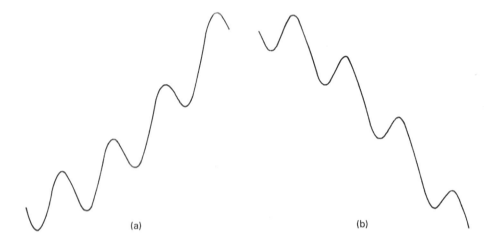

(a)   (b)

Figure 3.13   (a) Uptrend; (b) downtrend

it signals that the downtrend is coming to an end. Conversely if this inter-mediate cycle is just passing its peak, it will cause the uptrend to terminate, while for a downtrend the price fall becomes even steeper.

3. Head and Shoulders (Figure 3.14)

This pattern, which indicates that the share price has passed its peak, is formed by a combination of two cycles, one of which is about three times the wavelength of the other. The long term cycle is at or near its peak. The pattern is most symmetrical when the peak of the longer term cycle coin-cides with a peak in the shorter term cycle. The pattern becomes distorted as we move from this coincidence. A failure of the pattern occurs when the final leg does not turn down but turns up, i.e. the share price turns out not to have passed its peak. This would be caused by the intervention of another cycle which has just passed its trough as we approach the right-hand neckline of the formation. In a symmetrical pattern which does not fail, this intermediate cycle is either not present at that particular point in time, or is, like the major cycle, also at its peak.

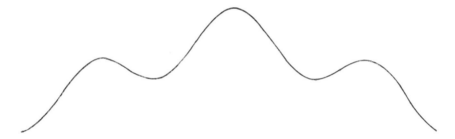

Figure 3.14   How a head and shoulders pattern is formed

4. Inverse Head and Shoulders (Figure 3.15)

This pattern, which indicates that a share price has passed its bottom, is formed by a similar combination of cycles as the above head and shoulders pattern, i.e. the major cycle is about three times the wavelength of the minor cycle. This time the long term cycle is at or near its trough rather than its peak. The pattern is most symmetrical when the trough of the long term cycle coincides with a trough in the shorter term cycle and, as above, the pattern becomes distorted as we move away from this ideal position. A failure of the pattern occurs when the right-hand leg does not turn up but turns down, so that the signal that the share price fall had come to an end was false. This failure would be caused by the intervention of another intermediate wavelength cycle which had just passed its peak as we pass

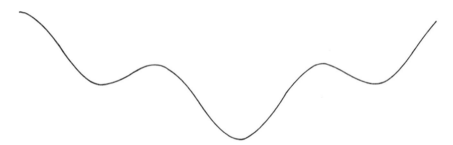

Figure 3.15   How an inverse head and shoulders pattern is formed

the right-hand of the two inverse head and shoulders peaks. In an inverse pattern which does not fail, this intermediate cycle is either not present at that particular point in time, or is passing through its trough at the same time as the major cycle.

5. Double Top (Figure 3.16)

This is caused by the combination of two cycles, one of which has about twice the wavelength of the other. For perfect symmetry the peak of the long term cycle must coincide with the trough in the shorter term cycle. The pattern fails if the price does not continue to fall after the right-hand peak is passed. As with other patterns that fail, the failure is caused by the intervention of an intermediate cycle which is just passing its trough, so that the upward surge in this causes the price to rise rather than fall. With a pattern which does not fail, the intermediate cycle is either not present, or is also passing through its peak at the same time as the major cycle, thus giving an added impetus to the fall of the price once the second peak is passed.

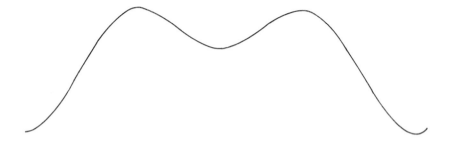

Figure 3.16   Double top formation

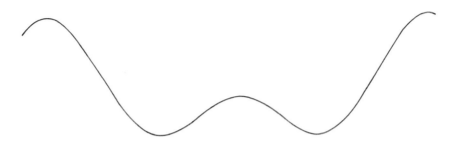

Figure 3.17   Double bottom formation

6. Double Bottom (Figure 3.17)

This is due to the same combination of cycles as the double top formation, except that the long term cycle is now at its trough. Again for perfect symmetry the trough of the long term cycle must coincide with the peak in the short term cycle. The pattern fails if the price does not continue to rise once the second bottom is passed. This failure is caused by the presence of an intermediate cycle which is just passing its peak, so that it then causes a downward surge in the price. The pattern does not fail if this intermediate cycle is either absent, or is passing through its trough at the same time as the major cycle.

We can see quite clearly from these examples that all of the favourite patterns that chartists use in their analyses can be explained simply by a combination of two cyclical trends that are in the right relative position to each other. It is the relative position of a third, intermediate cycle that is the major factor that decides whether the pattern will fail or not. If the intermediate cycle is not present the pattern will always succeed. If an intermediate cycle is present, the failure or otherwise of the pattern depends upon whether it is passing through a peak or a trough at the centre point of the pattern.

4

Isolating Trends from Complex Movements

In the last chapter we saw how trends of various periodicities or wavelengths could be combined together and combined with random movement to give composite movements. These movements are very similar to the movements shown by real share prices such as those shown in the charts in later chapters. Patterns that chartists rely on could be explained quite readily by the combination of two or more trends that had reached the correct relationship to each other, and those occasions where the patterns failed to complete their movement as predicted by the chartists could be explained either by the various cycles being only partly in the correct relationship to each other at the start of the particular pattern or by the intervention of another cycle.

The crucial question now is how far can we carry out the exact opposite to the procedures of the last chapter, i.e. from a historical sequence of a complex movement, can we firstly remove the random movement, and secondly isolate the particular cycles from which the complex movement has been composed? Of course this begs another question, and that is why should we need to do this in the first place? For share prices, the answer is that if we know the current state of important cycles in their movement, we will know at what point in their cycles the shares will be in the near future.

In this chapter we will be looking at simple methods in which trends can be isolated, as well as methods which are only readily carried out by a computer. The simple methods use either simple moving averages or graphical analysis.

It is much more informative to develop methods initially for artificial data, since the cyclicalities and amplitudes in the composite data are known. The wavelength of each component present will remain constant, and so will the amplitude. This means that it will be easy to verify if a method of resolving the various components is giving sensible results. We shall see in later chapters that share price data behave somewhat differently, since both the wavelength and the amplitude of a cycle can vary over the course of time. Even so, the techniques we develop using artificial cycles are valid for share price data, and the thorough understanding we gain by this approach will be invaluable for the real world of investment. We will be able to carry out procedures such as those discussed in the last chapter to predict how the composite movement of share price cycles will fluctuate over the near future. The many examples used later in this book will show how powerful these methods will be in determining the optimum buying and selling points for particular shares.

There are several ways of highlighting the cycles present in a complex movement, from simply drawing the smoothest line we can through the noisy data to the use of various mathematical techniques. The simplest and most easily understood of such mathematical techniques is the moving average method, which requires no more mathematics than the ability to add or subtract a few numbers, and we shall go into considerable detail on the effect of using moving averages on complex data.

A good starting point for developing a method of removing the random movement from complex cyclical data is to take a simple sine wave and random price movement combination similar to the one that we used in the last chapter. This was constructed from a simple addition of data which represented a random movement to data which represented just over half a cycle of a sine wave with a wavelength of 21 days. A period amounting to 40 days of this movement is plotted in Figure 4.1. The question is, therefore, that if we did not know that the underlying cyclical movement was one of a 21-day periodicity, can we still extract it from the data plotted in Figure 4.1? We can do this quite easily by the graphical method of drawing the smoothest curve we can through the noisy data, as is shown at the right-hand side of Figure 4.1. The smoothest line that we can draw freehand is fairly close in height and shape to the original sine wave that we started with. Therefore, quite clearly, the use of a freehand graphical method for extracting cycles from noisy data does hold out promise as a technique for analysing share price data, and this will be taken further later in this book.

The problem with a graphical method is that it is very subjective, and two investors may well come to different conclusions from the same set of data. A mathematical method, even a simple one, which takes the numerical data itself rather than depending on the graphical representation of the data, will avoid this problem, since the result of mathematical addition, subtraction, use of sines or cosines, etc., will always be the same. The use of such processes also holds out the possibility of developing an automatic microcomputer-based system where it is only necessary to feed in the daily or weekly closing prices of a particular share and the analysis then proceeds without the drudgery associated with extensive use of a calculator.

The easiest method for the investor to apply is the moving average method. Unfortunately, although many thousands of investors in this country routinely use moving averages as part of their investment, they

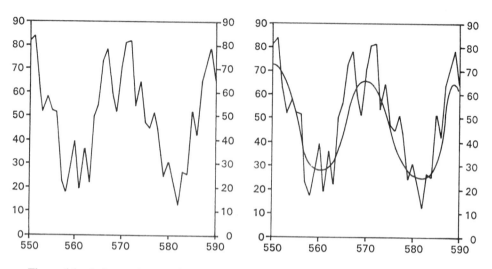

Figure 4.1 Left panel: a portion of a sine wave of 21 days' wavelength with random movement superimposed. Right panel: the same wave with the smoothest curve drawn freehand through it

have no understanding of what moving averages do to share price data, and simply use them in the outdated way used by the chartists for the last 50 years. They usually follow a set of rules such as "if the 10-day average rises above the 20-day average, it is time to buy", or "sell when the price falls below the 40-week average". We shall be showing in this book that such an approach to the use of moving averages probably throws away 90% of their power and only has an application as a selling or buying signal long after the actual peak or trough has passed. Using moving averages in the sense that we use them in this book puts the investor in the position of being able to anticipate buying and selling points, so that he is able to take action within days of the turn, many weeks before his rule-following counterpart above. Our investor will already be considerably in profit before his old-fashioned colleague can make up his mind.

CALCULATING A MOVING AVERAGE

Any average is calculated by adding together the values that have to be averaged and dividing by the number of such values. A moving average is calculated in exactly the same way, except that we have many more items in total than the number which we wish to average. In the case of the stock market we could average five consecutive weekly closing values to give a five-week average.

However, we may have available hundreds of weekly closing prices going back many years, and these will be added to constantly by the new closing value at the end of each current week. Taking the first five values from the set of data and averaging these gives the first average, but we can then move to the five values which start with the second data point in the sequence and calculate another average. We can proceed this way along the series until we run out of data. Since the operation moves through the data, the reason for calling such averages "moving averages" is obvious. The process can be illustrated for the data which gave the waveform plotted in Figure 4.1. The values in Table 4.1 represent 25 successive points in this randomised sine wave. The process can be somewhat simplified, since it is not necessary to keep adding five successive points and dividing by five to get each value for the average. A running total can be kept, and to compute the next average it is only necessary to add in the next point, and subtract the sixth point back (in the case of a five-week average), and finally divide this total by five. If longer averages are used, such as 31 weeks, for example, then the first 31 points are added and divided by 31 to give the average, and for the next value of the average the next point (the thirty-second) is added in to the total and the thirty-second point back (the first point in the sequence in this case) is subtracted from

Table 4.1   The calculation of a five-week moving average

Value	Subtract	Five-week total	Five-week average
49	x		
17	x		
18	x		
23	x		
60	x	167	33.4
61	x	179	35.8
50	x	212	42.4
49	x	243	48.6
61	x	281	56.2
64	x	285	57.0
71	x	295	59.0
82	x	327	65.4
50	x	328	65.6
69	x	336	67.2
76	x	348	69.6
43	x	320	64.0
32	x	270	54.0
48	x	268	53.6
40	x	239	47.8
30	x	193	38.6
30		180	36.0
16		164	32.8
38		154	30.8
50		164	32.8
36		170	34.0

the total before again dividing by 31 to get the next value for the average. The obvious place where the calculation can go wrong is in which value should be subtracted next from the running total. This is easily overcome by keeping a column where we tick off the last point which was subtracted so that we can keep track of what we are doing. It is suggested that you try the process of calculating a moving average on the data in Table 4.1 to satisfy yourself that you get the same results.

Now we come to a very important point about averages, and that is to determine with which data point a particular value of the average should be associated. The answer to this is that it has to be associated with the central point of the data which has been used to calculate the average. Taking the first five points which were averaged, then the resulting five-week average should be placed alongside the third point and not as we show it in Table 4.1. As far as calculating the average is concerned, this placement of the averages in the correct position does not matter since it does not affect the actual values in any way, but it does matter when we come to plot the average, and it will matter when we come to calculate the differences between the data and the average. We will see that all of our plots of moving averages superimposed upon data will be centralised in this way. By doing this, we will end up with similar plots to the freehand smoothing process we showed in the right-hand part of Figure 4.1. This point is clarified in the two plots in Figure 4.2 of the five-week average which we have just calculated in Table 4.1. The left-hand plot shows the average incorrectly superimposed, i.e. with the last calculated average value being plotted in the same time position as the last data point. The right-hand plot shows the data correctly superimposed so that any five-week average point is plotted in the same time position as the central point of the five values from which it has been calculated. The right-hand plot is obviously a "better" version of the noisy data from which it has been derived, while the left-hand plot has lost its time-based relationship with the original data. Note that the chartists, since they have no interest in the fundamental nature of moving averages or its relationship to the original data, plot them incorrectly as we have done in the left-hand part of Figure 4.2. If we look at moving averages as a smoothing device to remove random movement and highlight underlying cycles, then there is no question as to which of these two ways of displaying them has to be used. In general for an n-week average, which is better referred to as an average with a span of n weeks, we have to plot the average $1 + 0.5 \times (n - 1)$ points back in time, e.g. for a five-day average three days back, for a 13-week average seven weeks back, and for a three-year average one year back in time. Of course this formula only works properly with spans with an odd number, since for an even number we would have to plot the average so that its points lie *between* the original data points. Although this can be done, it is best to avoid the problem by using moving averages with an odd number of days, weeks or years in their spans. This restriction has no effect on our accuracy of prediction of share price movement.

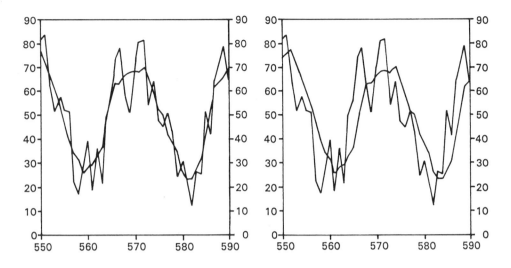

Figure 4.2 Left panel: five-week average incorrectly superimposed on the data. Right panel: five-week average correctly superimposed on the data

A consequence of plotting the moving average centrally is that we are missing some points at the beginning and end of the plot. In the case of a five-point average, we lose two points at either end. This is the penalty we have to pay for achieving a smoother (or "better") trace than the original, and of course means that with averages of very long spans, such as 51 weeks for example, we would be losing 25 points at either end. The mathematical reason we lose these points can be explained by looking at the calculation of the very first averaged point: we take five points, add them together and end up with just one averaged point. Therefore we have had to throw away four points in achieving this one average result, and we never recover these.

We will see later that this loss of data points leads to increasing uncertainty when we try to predict the current position of a cycle in stock market data as the periodicity of the cycles get larger. Thus we will know fairly accurately where a five-week cycle is this week, less accurately where a 13-week cycle is, and even less accurately where a 51-week cycle is this week, but even so these predictions are accurate enough for our purposes.

Note how successful a five-week moving average has been in removing random price movement and highlighting the underlying cyclical movement, since the original "noisy" data were composed of approximately equal amounts of a cycle of 21-week periodicity and random movement. The moving average method is able to cope with even larger amounts of random movement than that in this present set of data and so appears to offer a powerful method for highlighting cycles in stock market data, yielding smoothed data which has fewer fluctuations than the original.

THE EFFECT OF DIFFERENT AVERAGES

Before we can take this use of moving averages much further as a tool in cleaning up stock market data, we have to investigate the relationship between the span of the average in days or weeks and the cycles in the data which the moving average will highlight. After all, if we have say 250 weekly closing values of share prices, we can use any average from two weeks to 250 weeks, i.e. 249 different averages. It is important therefore to be able to know the grounds upon which we select any particular average and what we are trying to achieve by its use.

There are several mathematical consequences of applying moving averages to cycles of various periodicities, and these can be examined by using specific examples. Foremost of these consequences are:

- A moving average will completely eliminate cycles of the same periodicity as the span of the average.
- Cycles of lesser periodicity than the span of the average will be greatly reduced in amplitude, and may be out of step with the original cycles.
- The smoothed cycles will be of lesser amplitude than the original.
- Cycles of slightly longer periodicity than the span of the average will come through reduced in amplitude. The greater the difference between the periodicity and the span of the average, the less will be the reduction in amplitude.
- The greater the span of the average, the lesser will be the amplitude of the smoothed data.

To illustrate these above points, we can use the example of the 21-week cyclical data that we have been using previously. It will be necessary to use more than the 25 points used so far to show the effect of various moving averages. The pure waveform is shown in Figure 4.3, and this contains nine complete cycles of 21 weeks' wavelength. According to the first rule above, the application of a 21-week moving average to these cycles of 21-week wavelength should remove them altogether, leaving of course just a straight line.

That this is indeed the case is shown in Figure 4.4, where the data after applying a 21-week average to the waveform are plotted.

According to the second rule above, cycles of less periodicity than the span of the average should be greatly diminished and might end up shifted in time compared with the original cycles. To check this point on cyclical data of 21 weeks' periodicity it is necessary to use a moving average of span more than 21 weeks, say for example 31 weeks. The data after applying a 31-week moving average are shown in Figure 4.5. The most obvious point is that the smoothed data have about one-fifth of the amplitude of the original data, while perhaps not so obvious is the fact that the smoothed cycles are indeed shifted in time from the original ones, so that the troughs of the smoothed data coincide with the peaks of the original data, i.e. the smoothed data have been shifted by half a wavelength.

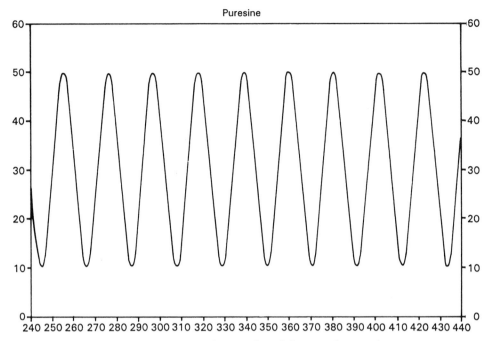

Figure 4.3   A waveform of 21 weeks' wavelength from peak to peak

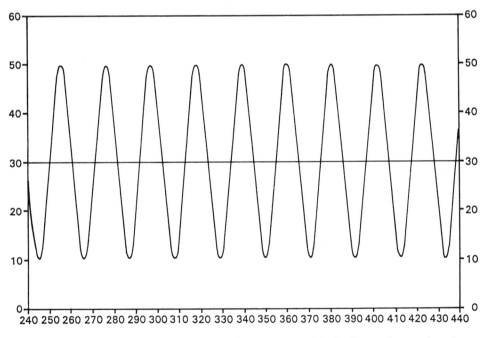

Figure 4.4   A 21-week moving average (horizontal straight line) superimposed on the 21-week cyclical waveform

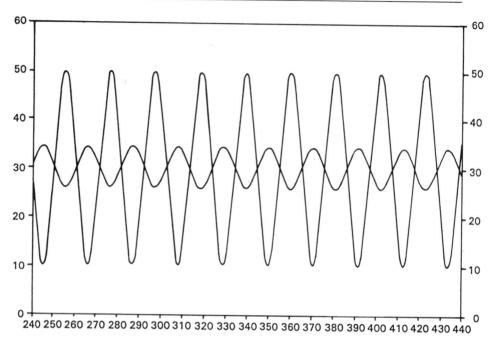

Figure 4.5 A 31-week moving average superimposed on the 21-week cyclical waveform. Note that, besides being greatly reduced in amplitude, the average is shifted to the right compared with the original waveform

Taking an even longer span for the average, for example 51 weeks, we get the result shown in Figure 4.6. The smoothed data are now even less in amplitude than was the result of using the 31-week average, but note that the original data and the smoothed data are now back in phase again, so that the peaks coincide.

We can look at two more examples of the effect of a moving average on these data, and that is to use spans of less than 21 weeks. The 13-week average of the cyclical data is shown in Figure 4.7. The smoothed data are once again of lesser amplitude than the original, and the peaks coincide in time. For comparison, a five-week average of the data is shown in Figure 4.8. Once again the peaks coincide in time, but now, as predicted in our rules, because the difference between the cycle periodicity and the span of the average is much greater than in the previous example, the smoothed data are much closer in amplitude to the original than was the case with the 13-week average.

These few examples help to clarify our ideas about what we can and cannot achieve by the use of moving averages. We have seen that by choosing an average with a span equal to that of the cyclical data, we remove this cycle altogether and end up with a straight line. We have seen also that the larger we make the span of the average, the smaller does the

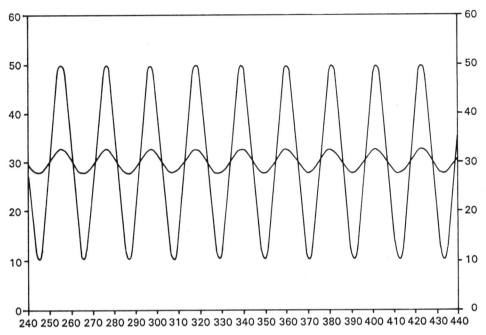

Figure 4.6 A 51-week moving average superimposed on the 21-week cyclical wave-form. Note that, although greatly reduced in amplitude, the average is aligned in time with the original data

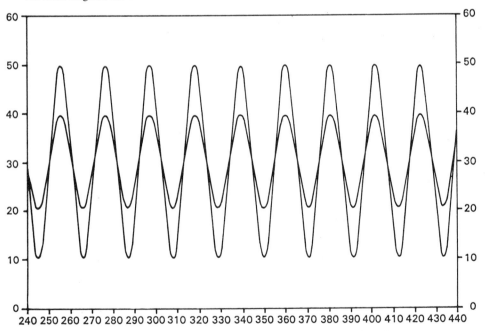

Figure 4.7 A 13-week average superimposed on the 21-week cyclical data

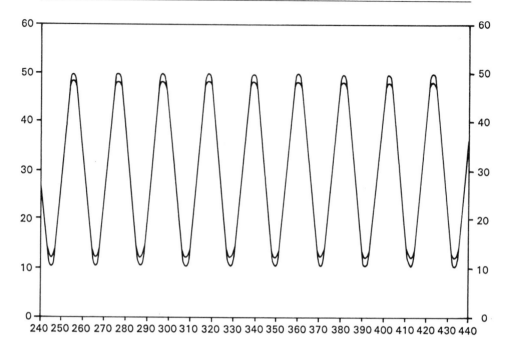

Figure 4.8 A five-week average superimposed on the 21-week cyclical data

amplitude of the resulting output become, and finally we have seen that we get unpredictable shifting effects on the cyclical data if we use averages of larger span than the periodicity of the cycles being analysed. Our conclusion should be from this that we should use moving averages of shorter span than the periodicity of the cycles in which we may be interested, so that to study say cycles of one year periodicity we should use a moving average with a span of say 31 weeks. There may also be occasions when we wish to suppress a cycle of a certain periodicity, and therefore we should use a moving average with span equal to this periodicity.

The more common cycles present in stock market data and the best averages to use to study them are discussed in detail in Chapter 6.

Now that we have explained in reasonable detail the effect of various moving averages on clean cyclical data, i.e. data which contain no random movement, we need to see what effect various moving averages will have on removing random movement such as that in the example plotted in Figure 4.1. As in the discussion above, we need to take a much longer timescale so that we see several recurring cycles within the data. Such a situation is shown in Figure 4.9, which represents once again data of 21-week periodicity with about an equal amount of random movement added in. The object of the exercise is of course to find the most appropriate moving average that will remove the random movement and leave the

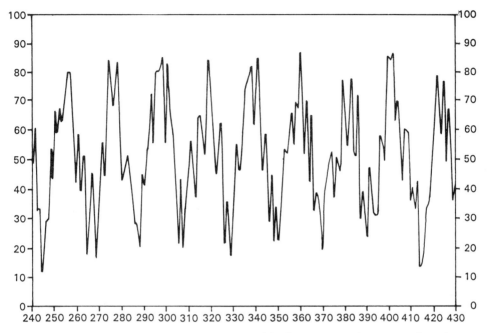

Figure 4.9 A 21-week cyclical waveform with about an equal amount of random movement added

cyclical movement highlighted and looking as close to the original "clean" waveform as possible, from the point of view of its amplitude, and with no shift in the time position of the peaks and troughs.

One restriction that we have already decided will be necessary is to avoid using an average with a span greater than 21 weeks, since the position of the resulting waveform is then not certain. The result of using five-, nine- and 15-week averages is shown in Figures 4.10, 4.11 and 4.12 respectively.

The trace in Figure 4.10, where a five-week average has been employed, while being closest to the original data in terms of the amplitude of the waves, still shows a considerable bumpiness. The 15-week average shown in Figure 4.12, while being much smoother, now has a greatly reduced amplitude compared with the original data. The best compromise is shown in Figure 4.11, where a nine-week average was used. The end result has only a little bumpiness on some of the peaks, but the amplitude is still about three-quarters of what it was in the original cyclical data.

From the above exercises on the application of moving averages to the analysis of cyclical data, with or without the presence of random movement, we can come to the following conclusion. *The most appropriate average to apply to a particular cycle is one whose span is about half that of the periodicity (wavelength) of that cycle.*

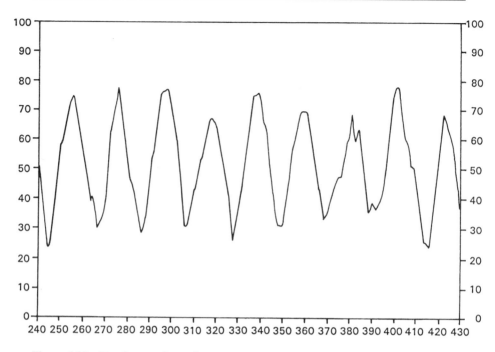

Figure 4.10   The five-week moving average of the data from Figure 4.9

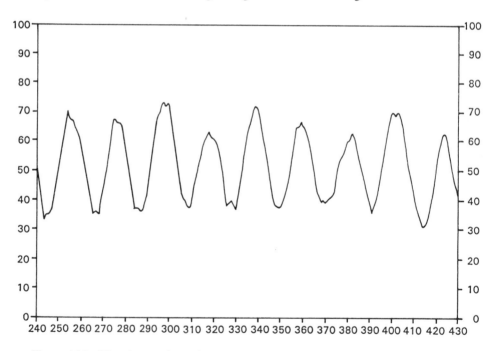

Figure 4.11   The nine-week moving average of the data from Figure 4.9

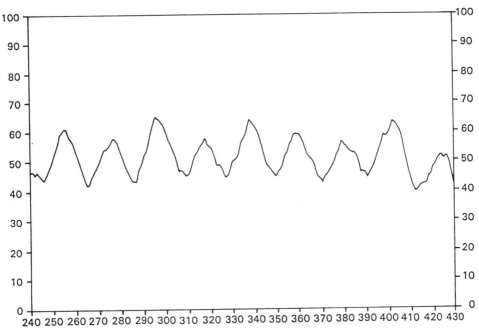

Figure 4.12 The 15-week moving average of the data from Figure 4.9

Now we can move to yet another complication, and that is how moving averages can deal with a situation where say two different cycles are present. If we can find out how to deal with such a position then we will be much better placed to apply moving averages to real stock market data. If we add in to the 21-week cycle we have been studying previously a longer term cycle, say of 51 weeks' cyclicality, then the trace shown in Figure 4.13 is produced. The challenge is to try by means of moving averages to isolate each of the two individual cycles, of 21-week and 51-week periodicity, from this compound data.

We have already stated that a cycle can be completely eliminated if we use the same span for the average as the periodicity of the cycle. It follows that if we use a 21-week moving average we should leave just the 51-week cycle in evidence, and if we use a 51-week average we will leave just the 21-week cycle, although in the latter case we run in to the problem that we may shift the position of the resulting output because of the effect we discussed earlier when the span of the average is greater than the periodicity of the cycles. We will also expect that the amplitude of the 21-week cycle will be drastically reduced. The result of applying each of these two averages is shown in Figures 4.14 and 4.15. The use of moving averages does therefore appear to work because in the two figures we can see quite clearly the two cycles in question, although they are diminished in amplitude from the original combination.

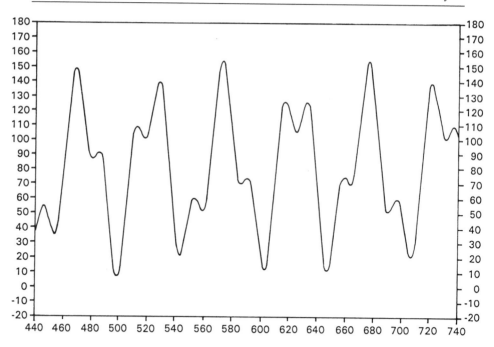

Figure 4.13   The effect of combining 21-week and 51-week cycles

It is interesting to see the effect of an intermediate span average, say of 31 weeks, on the same data. From the rules we deduced earlier, we would expect to see that the 51-week cycle would be the dominant feature, since this would not be removed by an average whose span was less than 51 weeks. We would also expect that the 21-week cycle would be considerably reduced in amplitude, and may have suffered a shift from its original position. We would expect to see the total picture as a 51-week cycle of rather lumpy appearance due to these remnants of the 21-week cycle coming through. Figure 4.16 shows that this is indeed what happens.

We should now have come to the conclusion that moving averages are an extremely useful tool for highlighting various cycles in data, although they are by no means ideal. An ideal mathematical process would eliminate everything except the cycle of interest, provided of course such a cycle was present in the data. Different cycles could then be studied by changing some parameters in the mathematical process. It is possible to get close to this ideal by the use of sophisticated digital filters, but the calculations involved are fairly heavy, and therefore only suitable for application where a microcomputer is available. The beauty of the moving average approach is that it is simple to use and requires no more than a

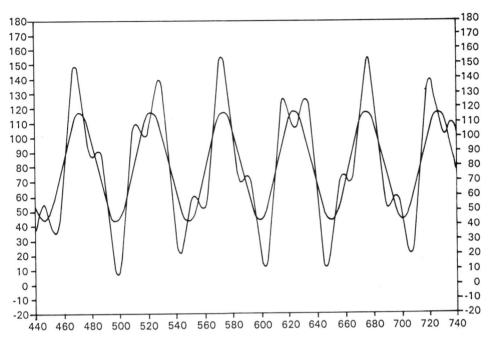

Figure 4.14 The 21-week moving average of the combined 21-week and 51-week cycles superimposed on the original data. The 21-week cycle is completely removed

calculator to work out the averages, although of course a computer does take the drudgery out of the process.

The drawback in the way we have been using averages so far is that they work in the opposite sense to the ideal mathematical process. They do not remove all cycles except the one of interest, but remove the one of interest and leave all other cycles, perhaps not intact, but certainly not reduced to zero. This means that to get information about a particular cycle in a complex mixture of cycles such as we get in stock market data would best be tackled by a process of elimination, trying various moving averages to eliminate cycles other than the one of interest. This would be a time-consuming process if it was not for one particular property of moving averages. *The data which we have removed in the smoothing process are still available.* These data can be recovered by using average differences.

AVERAGE DIFFERENCES

If we look again at Figure 4.2(b), we can see that of course the original data are scattered above and below the smooth line of the five-week moving average. In fact the data are randomly scattered about the moving average, and more importantly, this random scattering is identical to the

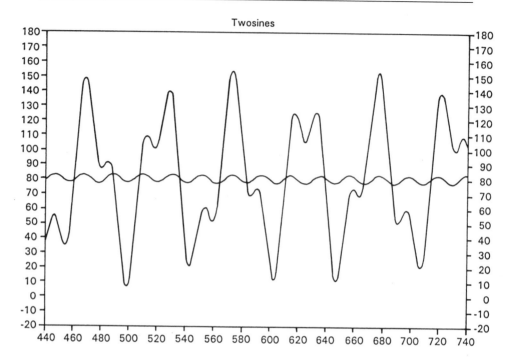

Figure 4.15 The 51-week average of the combined 21-week and 51-week cycles superimposed on the original data. The 51-week cycle is completely removed

random movement that we incorporated when we constructed the pattern from random movement and a 21-week cycle. The essence of this is illustrated in Figure 4.17. Since the random movement is represented by the distance above or below the smooth line of the average, then quite simply the random movement can be obtained by taking, at each point across the trace, the difference between the original data point and the value of the average corresponding to that point. These are the average differences which we will see are of great importance.

We pointed out earlier that the result of calculating an average should be associated with the point that corresponds to the middle of the span. The data in Table 4.1 were not aligned in this way since at that time we were simply concerned with how to calculate the values. It is imperative that the original data and the moving averages are correctly aligned before the differences are calculated, otherwise the results will have no meaning. The process of calculating average differences from the averages we calculated in Table 4.1 is shown in Table 4.2. The original column of five-week averages is left in and a new column with the same values placed alongside has been moved up by one less than half of a span, i.e. two weeks in this case, in order to align the data. This is done purely for clarity, and the investor can start off the moving average calculation by placing the values

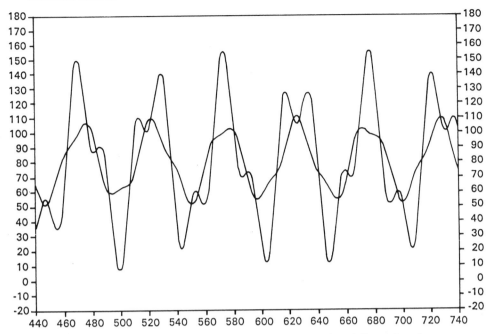

Figure 4.16 The 31-week average of the combined 21-week and 51-week cycles super-imposed on the original data

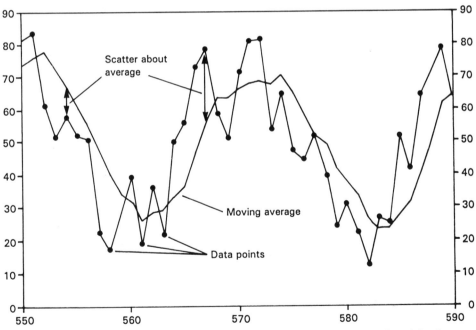

Figure 4.17 The random content of the original waveform is to be found in the vertical distance of each data point above and below the smoother average line

Table 4.2 Calculation of five-week average differences. Each moving average value has to be correctly aligned with the original data, i.e. placed opposite the central point of the span of the average. The first five-week average value is thus placed opposite week 3 and so on. The subtraction of the aligned average point from the data point can then proceed

Value	Subtract	Five-week total	Five-week average	Adjusted	Differences
49	x				
17	x				
18	x			33.4	
23	x			35.8	
60	x	167	33.4	42.4	17.6
61	x	179	35.8	48.6	12.4
50	x	212	42.4	56.2	−6.2
49	x	243	48.6	57.0	−8.0
61	x	281	56.2	59.0	2.0
64	x	285	57.0	65.4	−1.4
71	x	295	59.0	65.6	5.4
82	x	327	65.4	67.2	14.8
50	x	328	65.6	69.6	−19.6
69	x	336	67.2	64.0	5.0
76	x	348	69.6	54.0	22.0
43	x	320	64.0	53.6	−10.6
32	x	270	54.0	47.8	−15.8
48	x	268	53.6	38.6	9.4
40	x	239	47.8	36.0	4.0
30	x	193	38.6	32.8	−2.8
30		180	36.0	30.8	−0.8
16		164	32.8	32.8	−16.8
38		154	30.8	34.0	4.0
50		164	32.8		
36		170	34.0		

in this correct relationship immediately rather than in the way in which it was done in Table 4.1. The calculation then simply involves a subtraction, one point at a time, of the average from the data point with which it is now associated, as shown in the final column, and therefore is much easier to perform than the original average calculation which required an addition and a subtraction. Note that this final column may contain negative values.

Carrying out this process on the 21-week average which would have been calculated for the compound 21- and 51-week cyclical data, we get the plot shown in Figure 4.18. This should be compared with Figure 4.13 where we showed the 21-week average rather than its difference.

We can see in this comparison that whereas the normal 21-week average removes the 21-week cycles and allows through the 51-week cycles, the 21-week average differences allow through the 21-week cycle and any other cycles of shorter wavelength than 21 weeks. The reason why the plot is not now symmetrical is that traces of the 51-week cycles are still allowed

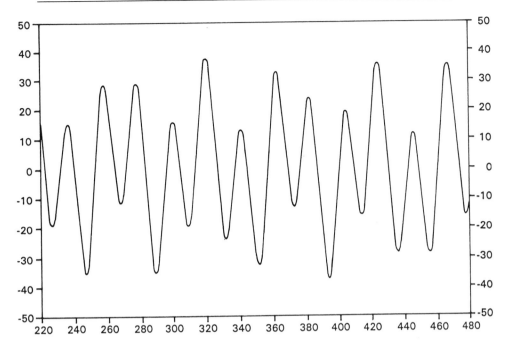

Figure 4.18 The 21-week average difference of the combined 21-week and 51-week cyclical data shows up the 21-week cycles even though their peaks and troughs are not aligned horizontally

through. The important fact, and this importance cannot be stressed too highly, is that the presence of a particular cycle can be confirmed by using these average differences. Thus in Figure 4.18, a check of the peak-to-peak or trough-to-trough distances confirms that these are exactly 21 weeks apart right across the nine complete waves that can be seen.

It is of interest to see the effect of applying a 51-week average difference to these same data, and the result of doing this is shown in Figure 4.19. We have now hit upon a problem, because a careful comparison with the original data shows that this new trace appears to be simply an inverted form of the original data, and we have had no success in highlighting one cyclical waveform at the expense of the other. The problem is the opposite to that which we found for normal moving averages, and can be expressed by comparing the two:

- *Normal moving averages allow through all cycles of wavelength greater than the span of the average, with the longest wavelengths being the least reduced. They eliminate entirely those with wavelength identical to the span of the average and greatly reduce those with wavelength less than the span of the average. In the latter case the waveform may be shifted in time. Moving averages eliminate random movement.*

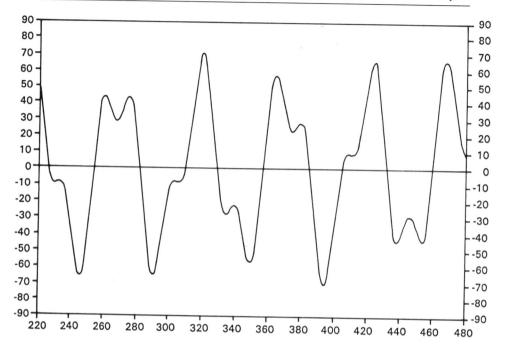

Figure 4.19 The effect of applying a 51-week average difference to the combined 21-week and 51-week cyclical data

- *Moving average differences remove all cycles with greater wavelength than the span of the average, allow through completely cycles with wavelength equal to the span of the average, and allow through cycles with wavelength less than the span of the average. In the latter case the amplitude will be reduced and the waveform may be shifted in time. Moving average differences will also allow through random movement.*

These two techniques must therefore be seen to be complementary, and can give extremely useful information if used together. Because this extra information is so useful, investors should adopt the policy of moving just this one simple level of calculation on from their normal practice of calculating the average and tabulating the differences. As with all the computational and display techniques discussed in this book, the MICROVEST 5.0 computer program (see Appendix) carries out this calculation rapidly and easily on daily, weekly or monthly data.

Probably the best approach to using average differences is to come to some idea of a particular cycle that may be influencing the current behaviour of a share price and to apply a moving average difference of that same span to the data. If cycles of that wavelength are not present because the peak-to-peak or trough-to-trough distances are not identical with this wavelength, then determine the wavelength of a cycle that may be present by measuring the distance between successive peaks and successive troughs. Now apply this value as the span of the new average differences to be calculated, and this newly discovered cycle should be enhanced.

As an example we may come to the conclusion that cycles of 31-week wavelength should be present in the combined data we have been using. Applying a 31-week average and calculating the differences gives the plot shown in Figure 4.20. If we measure the peak-to-peak or trough-to-trough distances, then it is obvious that these are not 31 weeks, and therefore we can say categorically that there are no cycles of 31-week wavelength present in the data. The peak-to-peak measurement suggests that there is a cycle present with a wavelength of about 20 weeks, and so it would be logical to apply an average difference of 21 weeks (bearing in mind a previous comment about using spans with an odd number of points). By doing this, of course, we get the plot we have already shown in Figure 4.18.

One final exercise is necessary before we leave this discussion of the fundamental way in which moving averages work, and that is to approach rather more closely to the real situation in stock market data by adding in random movement to the combined 21-week and 51-week cyclical data. The result of doing this is shown in Figure 4.21. Although it is obvious that there are cycles in the data, the random movement is now quite effective in masking the exact nature of the underlying cycles. Since stock market

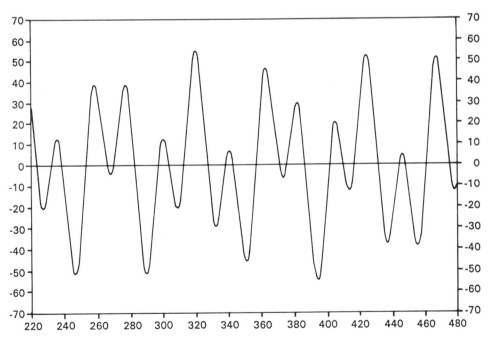

Figure 4.20 The 31-week average differences of the combined 21-week and 51-week cyclical data

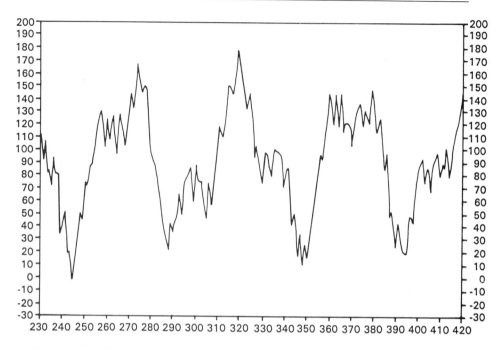

Figure 4.21   The combined effect of random movement with 21-week and 51-week cyclical waveforms

data will be more complex than these examples, it is essential that any approach we make in the application of moving averages has to be able to deal with data such as those shown in Figure 4.21. If we are not able to do this, then moving averages will turn out to be of little use in the real world of the stock market.

An understanding of the following logical approach is therefore vital, and the investor should re-read this section until he fully understands it.

Looking at Figure 4.21, we have no real idea of the underlying cycles that may be present, although the data do look cyclical in nature with a periodicity of more than 40 weeks or so. We should therefore try a moving average with a span less than this 40 weeks in order to allow cycles of 40 weeks to come through. A 31-week average is a useful one to try since it often gives good results in the case of share prices. The 31-week average is shown in Figure 4.22, superimposed upon the original data from which it is derived. We can see that this average is a reasonably regular waveform, although it is a bit lumpy and bumpy. This is due to the presence of other cycles in the data. A measurement of the trough-to-trough and peak-to-peak distances gives values of 57, 48 and 58 weeks for the troughs and 44, 58 and 46 weeks for the peaks. In a case like this, where the moving average is not too distorted and its amplitude is fairly constant, it is in order to take an average of these distances. This gives us (57 + 48 + 58 + 44 + 58 + 46)/6 =

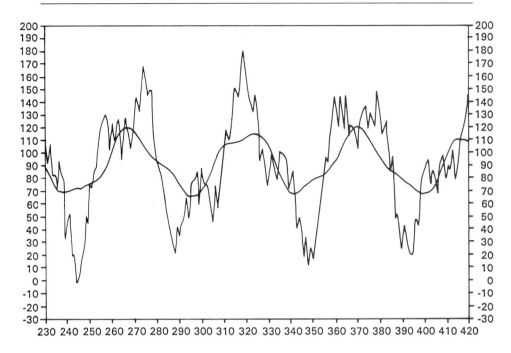

Figure 4.22 The 31-week average superimposed on the complex waveform from Figure 4.21

51.8 weeks. We can take this as a strong indication that we have a cycle of 51 or 52 weeks' periodicity present in the data, this cycle being distorted by the presence of others of shorter wavelength. We discount the presence of cycles of longer wavelength than 51 to 52 weeks because these would come through the averaging process unaffected, and therefore would cause the amplitudes of the averaged data to be distorted very much more than is the case.

As far as cycles of shorter wavelength than 51 to 52 weeks are concerned, the bumpiness of the average is fairly gentle, so that we can discount cycles of wavelength less than say 11 weeks. Looking at Figure 4.21 again, it is obvious that there is plenty of movement of only a few weeks' duration present. Since there is no sign of such fluctuations, even greatly reduced in amplitude, in the 31-week average, we come to the conclusion that these very short term fluctuations are random in nature, since of course random movement is virtually completely removed by a moving average.

Taking stock of what we have deduced so far, we can say:

- The longest cyclicality present has a wavelength of 51 or 52 weeks.
- Because of distortion of the periodicity but not of the amplitude of these 51- to 52-week cycles passed by the average, there must be cycles of shorter wavelength present in the data.

- Because the 31-week average is fairly smooth, these other cycles are not of very short wavelength.
- Since short term cycles are not present, the very short term fluctuations present in the data are due to random movement.

Now we can move to a consideration of the shorter term cycles that we deduced must be present in the data. Since we have already calculated the 31-week average, it is only one more step to calculate the 31-week average differences. The result is shown in Figure 4.23. Previous versions of average differences were smooth due to the examples being free of random movement. The random movement present in this example will come through the average difference process because all cycles of 31 weeks' or less periodicity are allowed through. Random movement is a special case with no periodicity. Thus the final result is seen to be noisy. In spite of this, at least we can try to determine the peak-to-peak and trough-to-trough distances in order to determine the wavelength of the cycle which is allowed through. These distances average out at about 21 weeks, giving an indication of the presence of cycles of this periodicity. This is about as far as we can go in deductions from the 31-week average and the 31-week average difference, our conclusion being that we have cycles of about 51 to 52 weeks' and 21 weeks' wavelength present in the data together with additional random movement.

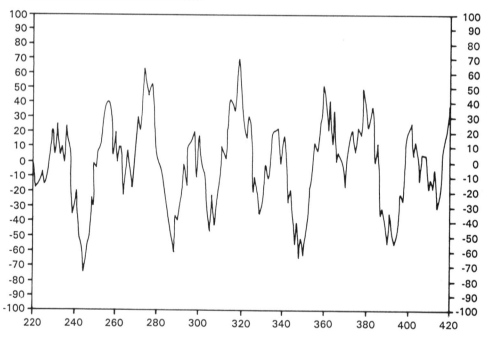

Figure 4.23 The 31-week average difference of the complex waveform from Figure 4.21

The next obvious step is to use a 21-week average, because this can be used to eliminate the suspected 21-week cycle altogether, leaving a much clearer picture of the suspected 51- to 52-week cycle which we think is present. In addition, by using a 21-week average difference, we will be able to highlight the 21-week cycle if this is indeed present.

The 21-week average of the data is shown in Figure 4.24. We can now see how successful the moving average approach is because a clean, uniform cycle is highlighted. Measurement of the peak-to-peak and trough-to-trough distances shows these to be consistent at 51 weeks across the whole plot. We have therefore been able to isolate the undistorted 51-week cycle that was present in the original complex data.

It will not be quite so easy when it comes to a way of isolating the 21-week cycle. A plot of the 21-week average difference will highlight the 21-week cycle if it is there, but unfortunately will also allow through the random movement, so that the net result may not be as useful as one would hope. This did not happen with the previous examples because they did not contain random movement. That there is a problem with noise is shown by the plot of the 21-week average difference shown in Figure 4.25. We need a method of removing this random noise from the 21-week average difference so that the 21-week cycle is much better defined.

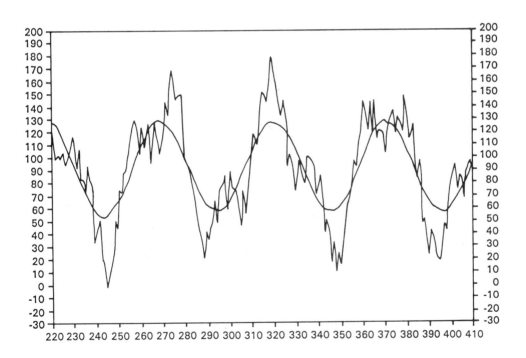

Figure 4.24 The 21-week average superimposed on the complex waveform from Figure 4.21. A clear, undistorted 51-week cycle is now visible

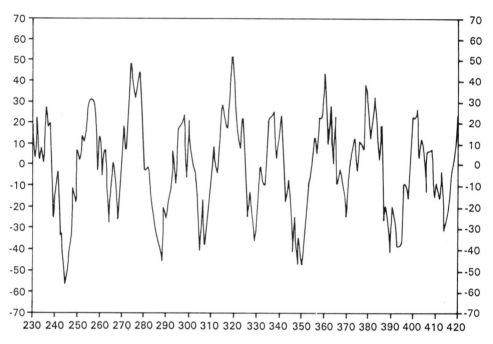

Figure 4.25 The 21-week average difference of the complex waveform from Figure 4.21

The solution to this should now be apparent, since we have been using the normal moving average to remove such random fluctuations. Therefore it would seem that applying a normal moving average to the 21-week average difference should do the trick. Of course, this means that we will have to carry out another layer of calculation, but this will be a small price to pay for solving this particular problem.

COMPUTER METHODS OF TREND ISOLATION

Up to this point, the methods of trend isolation are ones which, although perhaps tedious, are simple to carry out using just a calculator, and gave a great deal of information about the underlying trends in the data.

The main disadvantage of simple moving averages is that they are not very efficient at removing all shorter term fluctuations from the data. By using more intensive calculations, such as smoothing of simple averages by using a second average and especially weighted averages, a greatly improved performance can be achieved. Because of their intensive nature such calculations can only realistically be carried out by computer.

As far as the noisy data in Figure 4.25 are concerned, it only remains to decide which second moving average should be applied. One average

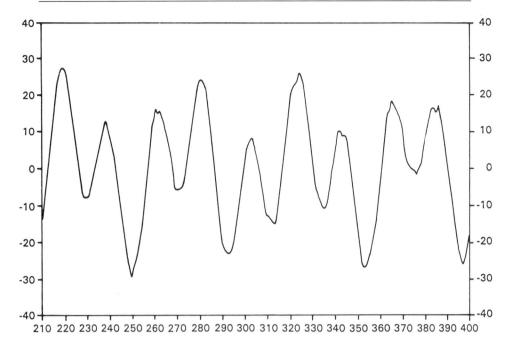

Figure 4.26 The 21-week difference of Figure 4.25 smoothed by the further application of an 11-week average. The 21-week cycles are now clearly observed

which we should definitely not apply is a 21-week average, since this will eliminate entirely the 21-week cycle from the previously calculated 21-week average difference. We noted earlier that an average of about half the span of the cycle we are interested in is the most useful average to apply. For smoothing the 21-week average differences, therefore, an 11-week average would be the best. The result of applying this second average to the data is shown in Figure 4.26. The approach has been successful in removing the noise from the 21-week average difference.

If we measure the peak-to-peak and trough-to-trough distances of these highlighted cycles, we find that they are consistently 21 weeks apart. Although there is a slight distortion in the amplitude of the peaks and troughs due to some carrying through of the 51-week cycle, we have now isolated the 21-week cycle.

So far, therefore, from a complex mixture of 51-week and 21-week cycles plus added random movement, we have been able to isolate each of the two cycles. It is of interest to see if we can put the final piece back into the jigsaw, and that is of course to determine what the random movement is. By definition, random movement is movement that has no periodicity and therefore will be unaffected by the average difference process. Since the average difference will remove cycles of longer periodicity than the span of the average, we should use as small a span as possible to remove all

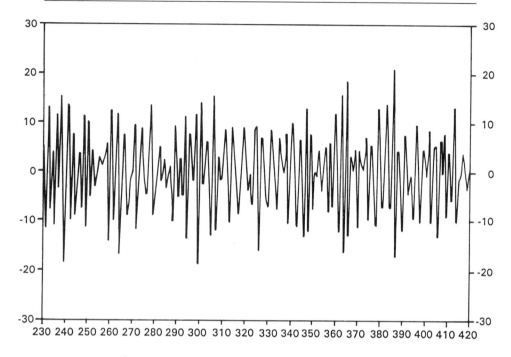

Figure 4.27 The three-week average difference of the original data from Figure 4.21 removes cycles of more than three weeks' wavelength, and leaves behind the random movement

cyclical data. Since we have been using simulated weekly data, the shortest span we can use is therefore three weeks since we have been using averages of odd span in all our examples for reasons discussed earlier. The result of doing this is shown in Figure 4.27. As we can see, this figure shows an obvious random movement with fluctuations of extremely short term being present.

It is now worth outlining the various stages which were applied to the complex mixture of 51-week, 21-week and random movement in order to isolate each component separately:

1. The 31-week moving average suggested an imperfect 51- to 52-week cycle.
2. The 31-week average difference suggested the presence of a 21-week cycle.
3. The 21-week average totally eliminated the 21-week cycle, thereby isolating the clean 51-week cycle.
4. The 21-week average difference isolated an imperfect (noisy) 21-week cycle.
5. The 11-week normal average totally eliminated the noise of the Stage 4 process, thereby isolating the clean 21-week cycle.

6. The three-week moving average difference totally eliminated all cycles of greater than three weeks' periodicity, thereby isolating the random noise.

By such a straightforward, sequential and logical approach we will be able to discover an enormous amount of information on the cycles which are present in the movement of a particular share price and particularly on the current state of those cycles.

The improvement which we saw in the average difference when a second average was applied can be taken a stage further by applying a second smoothing average to the original average rather than the average difference. As an example, in Figure 4.28 is presented a plot similar to that shown previously in Figure 4.1. Here we show the centred 31-week average of the same data and a smoothed, centred 31-week average. The smoothing is obtained by using a second average with about half the span of the first, i.e. a 15-week average. The positive effect of the smoothing is that the kinks in the simple average caused by the inefficient removal of the short term random fluctuations are removed. The negative effect is that the smoothed average terminates a total of half of the span of the first average plus half of the span of the second average, a total of 22 weeks, before the last data point of the set. This can be compared with the

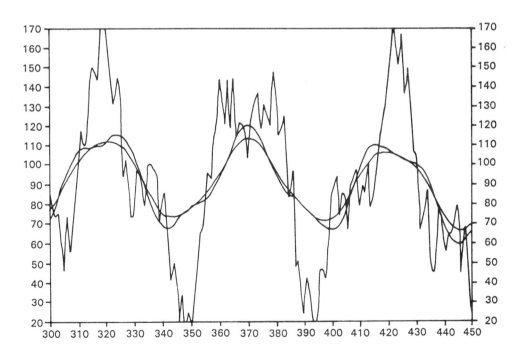

Figure 4.28 Comparison of a simple centred 31-week moving average and a smoothed centred 31-week average

simple average which terminates half of the span of the first average, i.e. 15 weeks back in time. Thus the penalty for giving a smoother and hence more predictable average is that we have to predict the future behaviour of the average over a longer period of time.

It is possible to improve the position shown in Figure 4.28 considerably by using a weighted moving average. This is calculated by multiplying each of the data points, for example 31 in this case, by a matrix of constants whose values have been calculated as being optimum for the particular average being used. This gives the first average point. The whole matrix is then moved down one place in the set of data points and the exercise repeated to give the next average, and so on until all the data have been used. It is obvious now why a computer represents the only realistic way in which this process can be carried out. The result of applying such a 31-week weighted average is shown in Figure 4.29. We can see that the result is better than that achieved with the smoothed average in Figure 4.28, and the average now does not suffer the loss of an additional set of points, terminating at the same point as the simple average.

Another method derived from the application of weighted moving averages is the cycle highlighter. In this case cycles of a nominal frequency, i.e. within a narrow window either side of a chosen frequency, can be isolated. Selecting a 51-week cycle as the one to be isolated from the complex

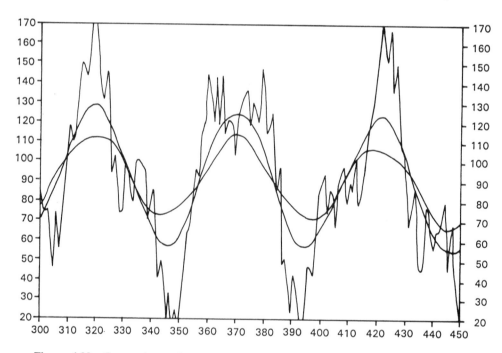

Figure 4.29 Comparison of a smoothed centred 31-week moving average and a weighted centred 31-week average

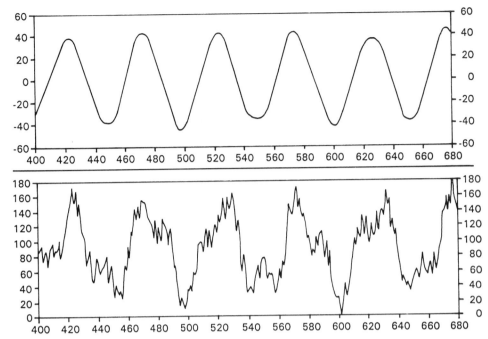

Figure 4.30 Using a cycle highlighter, the upper box shows a clean extraction of the 51-week cycle from the original data in the lower box

waveform shown earlier in Figure 4.21 gives the result shown in Figure 4.30. We can see that this is now a beautifully clear picture of the original 51-week cycle that was present in the data. The amplitude of the original 51-week cycle from which the data were constructed was 100, whereas the amplitude of the extracted cycle is 80. Thus there has been a small loss in amplitude caused by the extraction process because this involves moving averages. The amplitude loss is a small price to pay for the clear indication of the presence of an undistorted 51-week cycle.

One slight drawback of the cycle highlighter is the fact that longer wavelength cycles than the one being requested will still come through, albeit greatly attenuated. This can be shown in Figure 4.31 where an extraction of the 21-week cycle has been requested. Quite obviously, the resulting waveform is not as pure as was the case with the 51-week cycle. The trace is very similar to that shown in Figure 4.26, due to a residual influence of the 51-week cycle coming through the cycle isolating process. Even so, the presence of a 21-week cycle is very obvious, and from this its status at the time of asking, i.e. whether it is rising or falling, is easily determined.

This cycle highlighting method gives us a powerful means of predicting the state of selected cycles in the near future and leads to a composite picture of the movement of the share price itself.

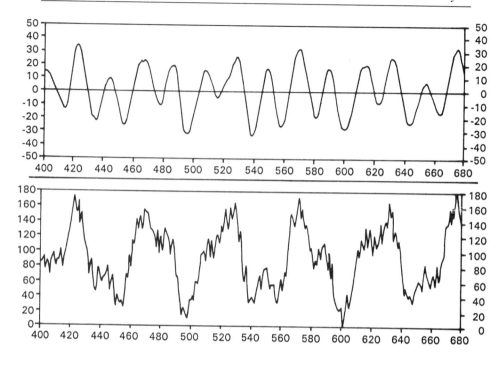

Figure 4.31 Using a cycle highlighter, the upper box shows the presence of a 21-week cycle in the original data in the lower box. There are still indications of the presence of a 51-week cycle

GRAPHICAL METHODS OF ANALYSING COMPLEX DATA—CHANNEL ANALYSIS

We pointed out the advantages of the computational methods of looking at cycles in share price data at the beginning of this chapter. These methods lend themselves to automation and graphical presentation by microcomputer and of course give consistent results. On the other hand, without the availability of a computer, the task of computing averages for large numbers of shares can be quite daunting unless the process has already been in operation for some time. The graphical method, while somewhat less accurate, has the advantage that once charts of the share prices of interest are available, it can be carried out quite quickly and some decision as to the future share price movement can be arrived at. The method is subjective, and therefore some practitioners will get better and more consistent results than others, but even the less expert of them will improve their investment performance beyond recognition.

Just as the foregoing moving average methods enabled us to determine which cycles were present in data, then so will a properly applied graphical method. A useful starting point is to take the combined 21-week and 51-week cycles illustrated in Figure 4.13 that we analysed using moving averages, and see if we can arrive at a similar conclusion as to the existence of 21-week and 51-week cycles in the data.

The method depends upon drawing a constant depth channel that will enclose the fluctuations in the data. Troughs in the data should touch the lower boundary of the channel while peaks in the data should touch the upper boundary. In the case of quite irregular data, it is acceptable to have one or two peaks or troughs penetrating the boundaries slightly. Boundaries may be adjusted inwards or outwards to arrive at this ideal situation. Since the combined 21-week and 51-week cycles as shown in Figure 4.13 are smooth and the peaks and troughs fairly regular, this will be an easier exercise than when we move to data which contain random movement. Note the important point that will be more relevant when we come to share price data, and that is that the vertical scale of all charts has to be linear. A good many chartists use a logarithmic price axis, and such an axis means that a channel of constant price difference would become narrower vertically as we move further towards the top of the chart. This is not acceptable for channel analysis. Logarithmic charts are used because they can display a greater price range than linear charts because of this compression at the higher prices, so they do have a use in share price presentation. All the charts in this book will be of linear form.

Figure 4.32 shows how the channel should be drawn so as to enclose the data from Figure 4.13. Several observations can be made to help in proper placement of the channel boundaries:

- The trough or peak of a channel does not have to coincide exactly with a major trough or a major peak. In fact, in a case such as this example, there will only be coincidence if the major peak or trough is symmetrical, or near coincidence if the peak or trough is nearly symmetrical, such as the major peak at 321 weeks.
- A consequence of maintaining a constant depth to the channel is that the peak of a channel will be offset to whichever side of the major peak the nearest minor peak has occurred. In the case of the major peak at 321 weeks, the minor peak on its left shoulder is slightly closer to the 321-week centre than the minor peak on the right-hand shoulder. The channel peak will therefore be at a point slightly less than the 321-week point. Taking a more extreme example, the major peak at 362 weeks has no minor peak on its rising left-hand side, but it does have a minor peak on its falling right-hand side. The peak point of the channel will therefore be quite a few weeks later than 362 weeks.
- The same argument applies to troughs in the channel. Thus the trough of the channel near the major trough at 290 weeks will occur a few weeks later due to the occurrence of the minor trough on its rising right-hand side. By the same token the channel trough near to the major trough at

246 weeks will occur a few weeks earlier due to the existence of the minor trough on its falling left-hand side.

• It is not the width of the channel as measured by the shortest distance between the boundaries, i.e. the line which would be at right angles to each boundary, that has to be kept constant. It is the *vertical* distance between the boundaries. Drawing channels in this way will give the illusion that the boundaries are not parallel, because the channels appear narrower at points where they rise or fall rapidly, and wider where they move sideways. Drawing constant width channels will be unsuccessful in isolating the cycles present in the data.

The forcing of the peaks and troughs to the right or left of the major peaks or troughs has the result that a more symmetrical channel will be produced than is shown by the symmetry of the underlying major peaks. We can see by close observation of the way that the channel has been drawn in Figure 4.32 that the boundaries now have an obvious cyclicality. The channel peak-to-peak distance and the channel trough-to-trough distance are virtually the same, and are 51 weeks plus or minus one week deviation to allow for measurement and drawing inaccuracy.

Thus, by graphical channel analysis, we have isolated the major 51-week cycle that is present in the data!

It is of interest to see how accurate we are in determining the positions of the peaks of these 51-week cycles, since we know where they are in the

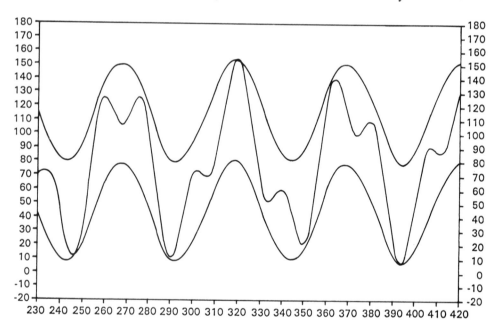

Figure 4.32   A channel drawn so as to enclose the data from Figure 4.19

original cycles which were incorporated into the complex data. From the channel drawn in Figure 4.32, we can find that the channel peaks are at 267, 319 and 368 weeks. In the original data these peaks were at 268, 319 and 370 weeks. We have been able therefore to establish the peaks and troughs of the underlying 51-week cycle to within two to three weeks!

We now have to discover a way of isolating the 21-week cycle which we know to be present in the data. We might at first think that by marking the positions of each of the troughs and measuring the distance between them we will arrive at a value of 21 weeks for this inter-trough distance, and by measuring the positions of each of the peaks we will arrive at the same value for the inter-peak distance. This unfortunately is not the case, since taking the first four troughs, for example, we will find that they occur at 246, 268, 288 and 306 weeks. These positions give inter-trough distances of 22, 20 and 18 weeks, so we can see that they are not consistent. *However, the points at which a successive trough and peak (or peak and trough) touch the outer channel are at a consistent distance apart.* These points are quite clearly seen in Figure 4.32, and a measurement of them yields a constant 11 weeks, i.e. a full cycle of 22 weeks. Thus, allowing for a one-week error in our drawing, we have also been able to find by the same graphical analysis the 21-week cycle which is also in the data!

It is vital to establish whether the positions we have determined for the peaks and troughs of these 21-week cycles by this method are close to the positions of the troughs in the original 21-week cyclical waveform which was incorporated into the complex data. The touching points as measured in Figure 4.32 for troughs are 246 and 288 and for peaks are 257 and 276. In the original 21-week cycle, these troughs occurred at weeks 244 and 286 and the peaks at 255 and 276. We have been able by channel analysis to establish the peaks and troughs of the original 21-week cycle to within two weeks! This is astonishingly accurate for what is after all a freehand drawing.

This one channel which we have been able to draw freehand has therefore solved two problems in the sense that it has enabled us to discover the two cycles which were present in the data. It is obvious that the placement of the channel is crucial, and a small shift in either direction at any point will cause the consistent major peak-to-peak and major trough-to-trough distances to wander from their constant 51-week value; the same will happen to the touching points of the minor peaks and troughs within the channel, so that these wander from their constant 21-week value.

Applying channel analysis to the data presented earlier in Figure 4.21 is much more challenging, as can be seen from Figure 4.33. The approach to the channel analysis of noisy data such as these, and to actual share prices, is to start with the channel which encloses the minor fluctuations. The same rules apply as we outlined earlier, so that the channel must be made as narrow in a vertical sense as possible so that the majority of minor peaks and troughs are touching it. It is permissible to allow a few of these to poke

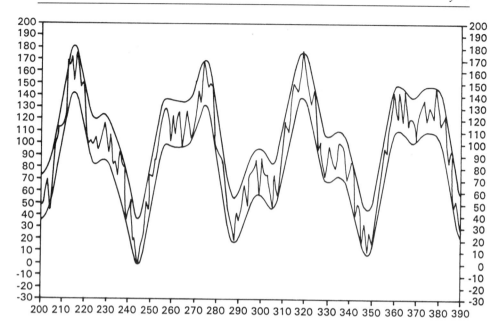

Figure 4.33   A channel drawn so as to enclose the data from Figure 4.21

above or below the channel. Since the channel has to be drawn as smoothly as possible, we may find that this restriction of limiting the number of occasions where the channel is penetrated will also reduce the number of points where the channel is just touched by the peaks and troughs, leaving many more well inside the channel and not touching it. It cannot be stressed too highly that the prime consideration is to achieve a smooth channel.

The fairly smooth channel that can be drawn by applying these rules is shown in Figure 4.33. The vertical depth is maintained at as constant a value as is possible by freehand drawing at a distance which corresponds to about 25 units of the left-hand vertical scale. At this point you should compare the shape of this channel with that of the data in Figure 4.13 which of course represented the combination of the 21-week cycle and the 51-week cycle *before* any random movement was added in. There is a striking similarity between the two as regards the positions of the peaks and troughs. This now tells us what we have achieved by drawing the channel: we have removed the random fluctuations from the data leaving behind only the combined 21-week and 51-week cycles. In other words channel analysis has behaved exactly like a moving average of short span in removing fluctuations of very short wavelength.

At this point of course our analysis is incomplete, since although we have removed random fluctuations, we still have no idea of the cyclicality of the channel that is left. The answer lies in the similarity of the shape of our channel in Figure 4.33 and the data upon which we drew a channel in Figure 4.32. We now have to construct an outer channel which will enclose the channel in Figure 4.33, applying the same rule about minimising the constant depth of this new channel and enclosing as much of the fluctuation of the inner channel as possible. In other words we forget about the random movements which have been eliminated, and treat the channel in Figure 4.33 as if it is the prime movement in which we are interested. This exercise is carried out in Figure 4.34. Note now the similarity in shape between this outer channel and the channel which we drew around the clean data in Figure 4.32. Because of this we will be able to apply exactly the same arguments to determine the wavelength of the two cycles which are present. Before we do this, there is one obvious point of difference, and that lies in the differing depths of the channel in Figure 4.32 and the outer channel in Figure 4.34. The reason for this is the presence of the random movement which forces a depth on to the inner channel. In Figure 4.32 this inner channel effectively coincides with the data and thus has a zero depth, because it contains no random movement in the data.

Applying the same analysis of the cyclicality as we did for the previous example, we find that the peak-to-peak distances and the trough-to-trough distances of the outer channel are 51 weeks, plus or minus one week to allow for inaccuracy in drawing the channel. We have therefore determined the wavelength of the major cycle in this complex data to be 51 weeks, which is exactly what it should be. Of course, this value of 51 weeks

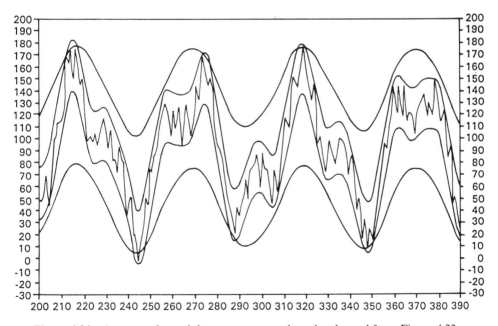

Figure 4.34 An outer channel drawn so as to enclose the channel from Figure 4.33

depends very much on the accuracy of drawing the channels. This accuracy can only develop with practice, and the investor is urged to carry out the above exercise himself by tracing the original data from Figure 4.21. With a badly drawn channel, the first thing that will suffer will be the consistency of the peak-to-peak and trough-to-trough distances, so that if you do not get these correct, look at your channel with a fresh eye to see which part of it might be distorted. Even so, channel analysis is fairly tolerant of drawing technique, and you will still find that although your distances are not all the same, taking an average of all the measurements will lead to a figure amazingly close to 51 weeks.

As with the last example, it is of interest to see how close to the real positions of the peaks of the 51-week cycles in the original data we have come with the channel analysis.

As far as the minor channel is concerned, again we measure the distance between the points at which the inner channel touches the outer channel. We will find that these distances are 21 weeks, give or take one week to allow for drawing inaccuracies. We have now been successful in isolating the second cycle from this complex data. The point can be made again that if the channel is inaccurately drawn, then these distances will not be a constant 21 weeks, but will vary somewhat depending upon how inaccurate the channel is. Even so, they should average out at a value quite close to 21 weeks, because as mentioned above, channel analysis is tolerant of considerable error in the placement of the channel boundaries. This error has much more importance when it comes to determining at what point we are on a particular cycle at a certain point in time. Thus although a badly drawn channel will still tell us that we have a 51-week cycle and a 21-week cycle present in the data, it might incorrectly be telling us that the 51-week cycle will bottom out at week 392 from the starting point of the analysis, whereas a more accurately drawn channel will tell us that the 51-week cycle will bottom out at week 386 from the starting point. As one can appreciate, a six-week error in pin-pointing the start of the new upward phase of the 51-week cycle would allow a considerable price rise to have occurred before our analysis told us that a buying point had been reached.

Having determined by channel analysis that we have a 51-week cycle and a 21-week cycle plus random price movement present in the complex data, there is still some vital information missing. This concerns the importance of each of these three components, i.e. their individual contributions to the overall final complex waveform. After all, when we come to real share price data, it will be of little use to spend a great deal of time isolating a particular cycle to find that it accounts for only a few pence of movement in the share price. We have to be able to determine the amplitude of the individual components of the waveform.

We noted in the discussion of moving averages that sometimes there was a considerable reduction in the amplitude of the cycles that came through the averaging process and sometimes these had been shifted sideways in time. This means that considerable care has to be taken in deducing the amplitude of the various cycles highlighted by the moving average process, although with this care good results can be obtained. With channel analysis, again by a careful approach, we can also get good results in the determination of the amplitude of the various components that are present. It is only necessary to discuss what happens when we draw channels in order to begin to see how this can be achieved.

The channel process is illustrated in Figure 4.35. Starting with a consideration of the outer channel of 51 weeks' peak-to-peak and trough-to-trough distance, i.e. 51-week cyclicality, we have drawn a centre line through the channel. This line represents the line that would be taken if no components of lesser wavelength were present, i.e. it represents the original 51-week cycle. The fact that the channel boundaries are a certain distance—about 50 on the vertical scale above and below this centre line—represents the additional movement forced on the 51-week cycle by the other two components, i.e. the 21-week cycle and the random movement. Therefore the act of just drawing this centre line has achieved two things. Firstly, the amplitude of the centre line itself, which is about 70 units on the vertical scale, is the amplitude of the original 51-week cycle. Compare this with Figure 4.14 where this cycle is isolated by the application of a 21-week average and you will see that the amplitudes are more or less the same. Secondly, the depth of this outer channel, about 100 on the vertical

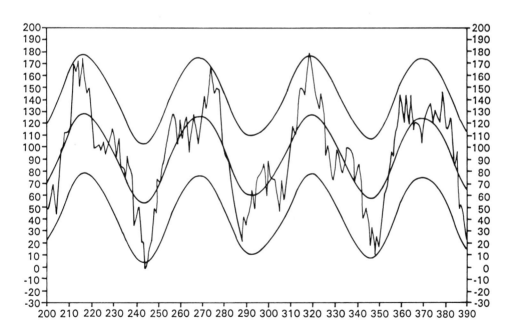

Figure 4.35 The centre line of the outer channel represents the original 51-week cycle

scale, is the combined fluctuation of the random movement and the 21-week cycle, free from the influence of the 51-week cycle.

Just as the centre of the outer channel uncoupled the fluctuations of the cycles of lesser wavelengths than that of the outer channel itself, giving us a value for the amplitude of the cycle corresponding to the outer channel and a value for the combined amplitudes of the other cycles, so we can repeat the process on the inner channel.

The line drawn through the exact centre of the inner channel represents the line that would be taken if no components of lesser wavelength than this inner channel were present. In this particular case, these components of lesser wavelength are the random movement we applied to the mixture of 51- and 21-week cycles to create the example in the first place. The depth of this inner channel is due solely to the random fluctuations. Since the depth can be measured on the vertical scale as about 35 divisions (Figure 4.34), we now have the amplitude of the random movement.

We have now reached the following position:

1. Total amplitude, measured by the distance from the lowest point to the highest point of the outer channel = 180 divisions.
2. Amplitude of the combined 21-week cycle and random movement, measured by the depth of the outer channel = 100 divisions.
3. Amplitude of the random movement, measured by the depth of the inner channel = 35 divisions.
4. Subtracting amplitude 2 from amplitude 1, we obtain the result that the amplitude of the 51-week cycle = 180 – 100 = 80 divisions.
5. Subtracting amplitude 3 from amplitude 1, we obtain the result that the combined amplitude of the 21- and 51-week cycles = 180 – 35 = 145 divisions.
6. Subtracting amplitude 3 from amplitude 2 (or 4 from 5), we obtain the result that the amplitude of the 21-week cycle = 100 – 35 = 145 – 80 = 65 divisions.

Just to show how accurate these values are compared with the original cycles and random movement that were added together to produce this example, we need to know the amplitudes of these original components. These were as follows: 51-week cycle—100 divisions; 21-week cycle—50 divisions; and random movement—40 divisions. We are therefore 80% correct with our estimation of our 51-week cycle amplitude, within 30% of the 21-week cycle amplitude and within five divisions or about 12% of the amplitude of the random movement. These are extremely impressive results for a graphical method, especially when we take into account our previous comments about the accuracy of our determination of the positions of the various cycles in time.

This gradual introduction to channel analysis has brought home the power of the method when applied to artificial data against which our results can be checked. Even though share price data may frequently contain many more cycles than the small number we have analysed in this chapter, and cycles which will also vary in both wavelength and amplitude over the course of time, the principles which have been discussed in the chapter are just as valid. The investor should now see quite clearly the relationship between the data and moving averages and the relationship between the data and the channels which we can draw on the data. As a result, the investor should now be in the position that he can understand which moving average or moving average difference should be chosen to highlight the particular cycles in which he is interested. No longer are these magic numbers conjured up by investment writers which appear to work most of the time. They are now fundamental values which have to be changed according to the circumstances.

In the following chapters, the investor will see exactly how powerful channel analysis is when applied to real stock market prices, and will also see the close relationship between channels and moving averages.

5

Predicting Future Movement

The last chapter was spent in the analysis of complex cyclical data and random movement, with the prime objective being to develop methods of separating out the various cyclical and random movements. We showed that by using either moving averages or channel analysis we could determine the amplitude of each waveform and where it was standing at the present time relative to its peak or trough.

The major reason for doing this, of course, is to enable us to predict where the combination of these known cycles will take us in the future. There are two main methods by which we can attempt this prediction. The first method is a computational one, while the second is a graphical one. The principle of the computational method is quite straightforward, but the calculations, while simple, are time consuming. For this reason it is only really practicable to use this method on a computer, and software packages to carry out these processes are available commercially (see Appendix).

The figures displayed in the last chapter were produced by a computer, and it is necessary to enter only three values for any particular cycle which is required for display. These are:

- The wavelength of the required cycle in days, weeks or years.
- How far along in days, weeks or years from a trough we wish the starting point to be.
- The amplitude we require for the cycle. This can be expressed in points for an index, as a simple number for an exchange rate, or in a currency such as pence/pounds for a stock price.

Taking the examples in the last chapter, we used two cycles, of 21 weeks' and 51 weeks' wavelength. The amplitudes used were 50 divisions for the 21-week cycle and 100 divisions for the 51-week cycle. Finally, a random movement of up to 40 divisions was also added in to give the complex waveform shown in Figure 4.20.

Having determined the positions of the various cycles at a certain point in time, and having determined their amplitudes, we can use these values in the computational process to project the combination of cycles into the future.

DETERMINING THE CURRENT POSITION OF THE CYCLES BY COMPUTATION

In the last chapter we looked at two main methods of determining which cycles were present in the data, and where the peaks and troughs occurred. In order to develop the discussion into the predictive aspect of the analysis, it is necessary to select some cut-off period as being the end of the actual data. Most of the figures in the last chapter showed the time axis in weeks, going up to about 400. It is useful, therefore, to take week 400 as being the last week for which any data are available.

Firstly, we can look at what moving average methods tell us about the position of the two cycles, which we know to be present, at week 400. The slight difficulty which we encounter when we use moving averages is the loss of data points at the beginning and end of the averaging process. As we pointed out in the last chapter, because we adjust the position of the average so that an average value is correctly associated with a data point, the $(n - 1)$ data points which are lost in calculating the average are divided equally between the beginning and the end of the data being averaged. The averages we used in the various examples in the last chapter were of 21-, 31- and 51-week spans, and in addition we applied an 11-week average to the 21-week difference. The loss of points at the end of the averaged data will be 10 for the 21-week average, 15 for the 31-week average and 25 for the 51-week average. The effect of this loss of points when plotting the recent values of the averages and the data up to a cut-off point at say week 400 is illustrated in Figure 5.1. Not shown is the effect of applying an 11-week average to the 21-week difference, but the effect is cumulative. In calculating the 21-week difference we lose the last 10 points, and in applying a further 11-week average we lose another 5 points. This means a total loss of 15 points. Naturally the application of further averages to already-averaged data, while yielding much smoother and perhaps much more significant results, will have a counterbalancing disadvantage in this loss of data points. The disadvantage is minimal in the case of these theoretical, clean sine waves we are using for the examples, because their regularity means that it is simple to project them into the future. With real stock market data, we will have an interesting conflict between the much smoother curves obtained by using longer span averages or multiple applications of an average which should make them easier to project into the future, and the larger amount of time over which the projection must be made.

Taking the 21-week average of the complex data which was shown in Figure 4.24, and assuming a cut-off point at and including week 400, we get

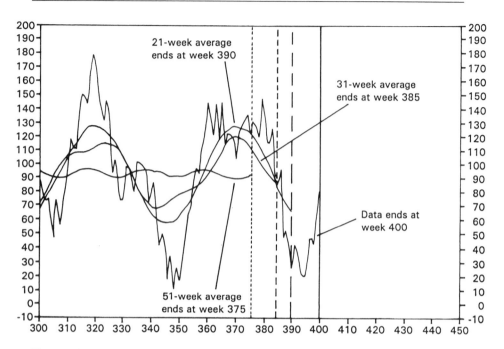

Figure 5.1 How various weekly averages terminate half a span of the average back in time. The loss of data points is the penalty paid for a "better" representation of the data

the position shown in Figure 5.2. The average terminates at week 390, i.e. 10 weeks back, but because the curve is smooth, it is easy to project it graphically forward up to and past week 400. To do this computationally, we simply need to determine the three items of data necessary for this exercise, and these can easily be abstracted from Figure 5.2:

• The wavelength. This is obtained by measuring from peak-to-peak along the time axis, and is of course 51 weeks.
• The amplitude. This is obtained by measuring from trough to peak along the vertical axis, and is 75 divisions.
• The current position in time of the waveform. This is determined by measuring from the last trough to the cut-off point at week 400, and is three weeks.

Thus we have a waveform which is three weeks past its trough, has a wavelength of 51 weeks and has an amplitude of 75 divisions. The cycle is now totally defined, and its position at any time in the future is known.

Note an immediate source of error, and that lies in the amplitude of the averaged data. Unlike graphical channel analysis, the application of moving averages reduces the amplitude from its correct value. We stated in the last chapter that the original amplitude of the 51-week cycle was 100

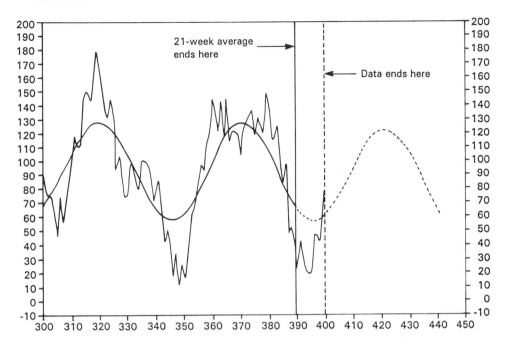

Figure 5.2 The 21-week average (which in this example highlights the 51-week cycle) terminates 10 weeks back from the last data point at week 400. Because of the regularity and smoothness of the average, it is easy to project it forward (dotted line) these 10 weeks to the time of the last data point and even well into the future

divisions, so that we have lost a quarter of this amplitude by applying the 21-week moving average.

As far as the 21-week cycle is concerned, the clearest picture we have of this cycle was achieved by using the cycle highlighter or by taking an 11-week average of the 21-week average difference. For the reason stated above, in the latter case this average terminates 15 weeks back from the 400-week cut-off point. In the case of the cycle highlighter, the computation terminates 10 weeks back from week 400. Thus the cycle highlighter gives the better information for computational purposes.

The required three items of data to compute the 21-week cycle into the future can be obtained from its plot in Figure 5.3:

- The wavelength. This is 21 weeks peak-to-peak.
- The amplitude. This is 45 divisions from trough to peak and is obtained by taking an average of the nine waves which can be seen.
- The time since the last trough. At week 400, the last trough was 31 weeks back at week 369. Since the wavelength is 21 weeks, the next trough should be at 369 + 21 = 390 weeks. This is at the last computed point for the cycle (due to the loss of 10 weeks in the computation). Thus the latest trough can be estimated as being 10 weeks ago.

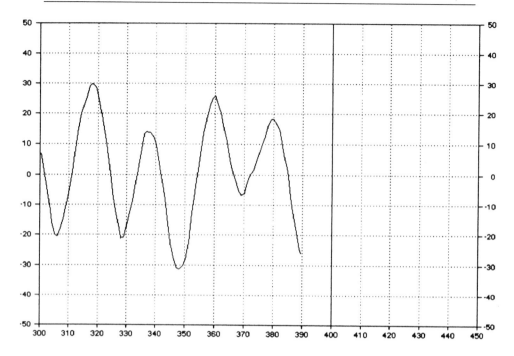

Figure 5.3 Isolating the 21-week cycle by the cycle highlighter. The random noise is eliminated. This leaves a smooth trace which finishes 10 weeks back from the latest data point at week 400, enabling the position of the troughs and peaks to be determined accurately

As was the case with the 51-week cycle, the amplitude is rather less than it should be, being 45 divisions instead of 50, but this is an acceptable error.

The last item we need in order to be able to reconstruct our composite data is the amplitude of the random movement. This random movement has no obvious wavelength, and consists of unpredictable movement on a week-to-week basis in the case of these weekly data. A very short term moving average such as three weeks or five weeks should remove this. Therefore we can display this removed random movement by charting the three-week or five-week average differences. This is done in Figure 5.4. The amplitude of the random movement can now be seen to be about 30 divisions.

PREDICTING THE FUTURE POSITION OF THE CYCLES BY COMPUTATION

We now have all the values we need to reconstruct our version of the original data by using the cycles and random movement which we have

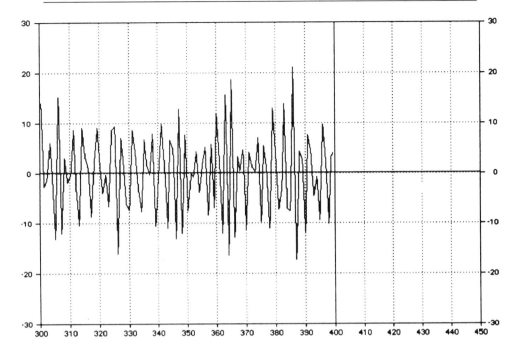

Figure 5.4 The random movement is isolated by taking a short term moving average difference. In this case a three-week average difference has been used. The plot finishes at week 399

deduced are present in these data. We have a reasonable expectation that our reconstructed data will look something like the original, although we also expect that the amplitude will be rather different because of the difficulty the moving average approach encounters in determining the exact amplitudes of cycles which are present in the data. We will, if you like, have determined a formula by which we can predict a value for the data at any point in the future. These reconstructed data will be obtained by adding together these three components:

- Cycles of 51-week wavelength and 75-division amplitude, starting three weeks after a trough.
- Cycles of 21-week wavelength and 45-division amplitude starting 10 weeks after a trough.
- Random movement of 30-division amplitude.

The result of doing this is shown in Figure 5.5. Since the highlighter used to compute this projected waveform terminated 10 weeks back from the cut-off point for the data at the 400-week mark, the projection has to start from that point, i.e. week 390 and not week 400. In other words, there is uncertainty in filling in the gap between week 390 and the cut-off point, and so this region has to be part of the reconstituted waveform. The most important feature of Figure 5.5 is that the general shape of the waveform is the same. We can take one complete wave prior to week 390 and find a corresponding calculated wave after week 390 that is virtually identical in shape, and differs only in its amplitude. Two such pairs of original and calculated waves are indicated in Figure 5.5. The amplitude of the calculated waves is about 75% of that of the original, so we can obviously improve our prediction of the waveform by increasing the values for the amplitudes of each component over and above the amplitudes we deduced from the moving average analyses. Although, of course, we could experiment by increasing the amplitude of the 51-week cycles, the 21-week cycles and the random movement in turn, it is simpler to adjust them all upwards by the same percentage. Increasing them by say a third, i.e. multiplying each amplitude by 1.33, should bring the predicted amplitude fairly close to the original. In Figure 5.6 we compare the portion of the original waveform between weeks 300 and 390 with the predicted waveform for a future portion between weeks 550 and 640. The amplitude of the predicted waveform is now adjusted by this factor of 1.33. It is clear that, while not quite superimposable, the two waveforms are almost identical.

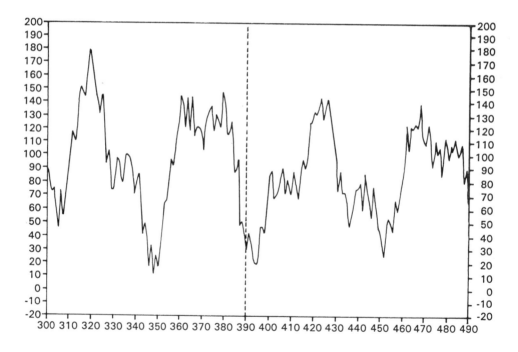

Figure 5.5 Actual data (up to week 390) and calculated data (after week 390) based on analysis by moving averages and recombination of the cycles and random movement isolated by the analysis

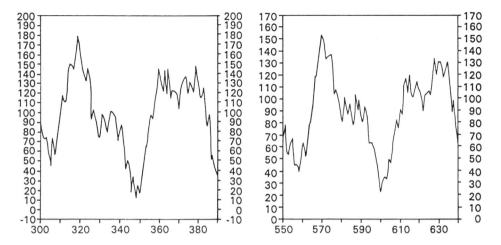

Figure 5.6 Left-hand panel: enlarged portion of Figure 5.5 showing the actual data from week 300 to week 390. Right-hand panel: predicted data from week 550 to week 640. The amplitude scale of the latter has been expanded to give the predicted wave the same amplitude as the actual wave

The reason that the predicted waveform is not exactly superimposable on the original is quite simple. It is because of the random movement that is present. The word random means unpredictable, and therefore we are never going to be able to predict exactly the future course of a complex waveform in which there is an element of random movement. The greater the amount of random movement that is present, the less accurate will be our predicted movement, whereas the lesser the amount of random movement, the more accurate will be our prediction. When it comes to shares, application of the moving average or channel analysis techniques will show us which shares are high in random content and which are low, so that it will be much more sensible to concentrate on the latter category.

Notwithstanding this difficulty, the general principle of deducing by various moving average calculations the cycles and random movement present in a complex waveform, and more particularly, where these cycles are in the overall time frame, with a view to recombining them to predict future price movement, is therefore a valid one, and in this computer age is ideally suited to automatic calculations with the minimum intervention from the user.

DETERMINING THE CURRENT POSITION OF THE CYCLES GRAPHICALLY

The above techniques are extremely powerful, and with the increasing availability of computers at reasonable prices are open to most investors who are prepared to spend a little time learning how to use them. However, as we pointed out in the last chapter, almost as good results can be obtained by the graphical technique of channel analysis. The best results are obtained by application of both moving averages and graphical methods to determine the best channels within which the data is oscillating, and the power of using both of these techniques will become obvious in subsequent chapters.

The starting point for channel analysis is where we left off in the last chapter, illustrated by the channels we drew in Figure 4.34. We were able to draw an outer channel which was fairly regular in shape and with the peak-to-peak and trough-to-trough distances being 51 weeks. Within that we drew an inner channel, and the important point was that points where the inner channel touched the outer channel were also fairly regularly, but not exactly, spaced in time. From this we were able to deduce the cyclicality of the second composite wave as being about 21 weeks.

In Figure 5.7 we show this analysis repeated for the data running from week 280 up to the cut-off point at week 400. The general approach in channel analysis is exactly the opposite for projection into the future as it is for establishing the channels for the historical price movement. In our introduction in the last chapter to the method of drawing channels for noisy data, we pointed out that we have to start with the channel that encloses the minor fluctuations in the data. Once this channel is drawn we can draw the next outer channel that encloses the fluctuations in the inner channel. If we have enough data we can then draw the next outer channel that encloses the fluctuations in this second channel.

A consideration of these historically drawn channels shows that by the very nature of the channel process, the outermost channel will be the smoothest, and therefore the most easily extrapolated into the future. The next channel in from the outside will be the next best to tackle, while the inner channel will be the least smoothest and therefore the most difficult. Thus historically we construct channels from the inside to the outside, but in future projections we construct them from the outside to the inside.

Looking at Figure 5.7, we can see that since the outer channel is so regular, both in shape and with the spacing of the peaks and troughs, it is an easy task to dot in the future movement of the channels, maintaining the same peak-to-peak distance, the same trough-to-trough distance and the same amplitude.

The task of projecting the inner channel into the future is a bit more difficult, but understanding the approach is vital if the technique is to be successful in the prediction of share prices.

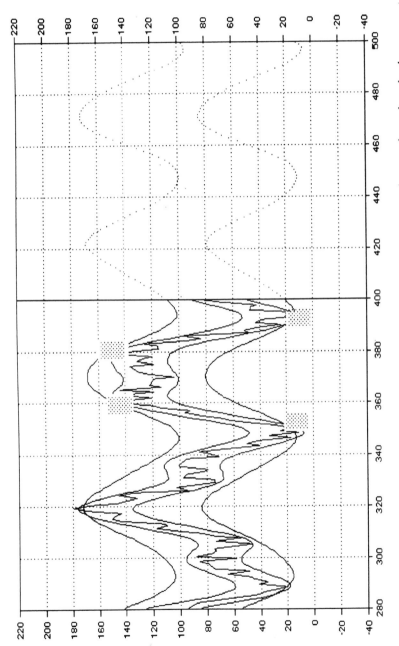

Figure 5.7 Once the inner channel has been drawn around the complex waveform, the smooth outer channel can be drawn so as to contain as much of the movement of the inner channel as possible. The greater regularity of the outer channel enables it to be projected into the future past week 400 as a dotted line. The channel touching points (hatched areas) are essential for predicting the future movement of the inner channel within the outer channel

The analysis depends on establishing for as many points as possible prior to week 400 those places where the inner channel touches the outer channel. In Figure 5.7 four of these points are shown as hatched areas, and prior to these there are another four places where this happens. The touching points that can be identifed are:

- Touching upper boundary: 299 320 341 362 383
- Touching lower boundary: 288 309 330 351

We would expect a touching point at week 372, but in maintaining the smoothest possible outer channel, we find that the data, while at an obvious trough at week 372, do not descend low enough to meet the boundary. The reason for this is that week 372 just happens to coincide with a particularly large upward random movement, and it is this which prevents the inner channel from touching at that point. We will find that in the analysis of stock market data, there are many occasions where the data do not touch the channel at the predicted point, but an attempt at touching the channel at a strongly predicted point, as in this case, can be counted as a positive. Because these touching points are so regularly spaced, we can predict where future ones should come. For the upper and lower boundaries, by continuing the regular spacing, these should be:

- Upper boundary: 404, 425, 446, 467, etc.
- Lower boundary: 393, 414, 435, 457, 478, etc.

Having predicted these touching points between the inner and outer channels for future movement past week 400, we can now begin to sketch in this inner channel to take account of this constraint which the outer channel places on the movement of the inner channel. The result is shown in Figure 5.8. The predicted upper and lower boundary touching points are indicated by the arrows. These arrows provide a useful guide for the estimated progress of the inner channel. Investors will find that the flexible curves or curve templates sold in stationers will aid this projection of channels enormously, giving not only a pleasingly smooth curve, but more importantly a pretty accurate one.

This inner channel is, of course, the channel that we have been aiming for in the whole process of channel analysis, because it is the channel within which we expect the complex movement to oscillate for most of the time, only moving outside this inner boundary on very few occasions. This is because we drew the channels in the first place with the restriction that the price had to stay within them with only a few excursions outside their boundaries being allowable, and this restriction will stay with us for the projected channel.

We cannot take channel analysis of these data any further than this inner channel, i.e. there is no inner channel to this inner channel, because now we are at the level where the movement within the inner channel is due totally to the random movement in the complex waveform. Channel analysis can only highlight the movement which is due to the presence of a particular cycle in the data.

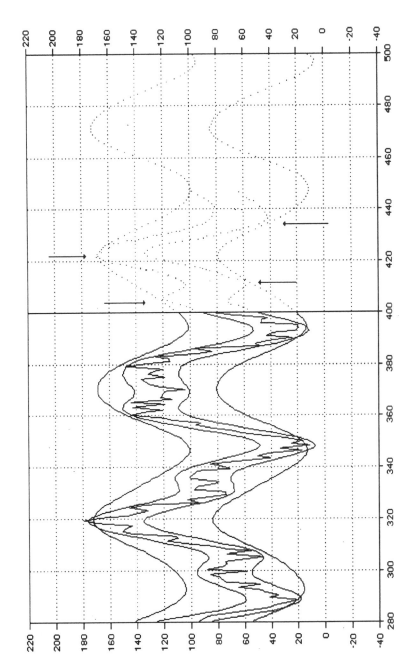

Figure 5.8 Projecting an inner channel past week 400. The outer channel has already been projected (Figure 5.7). The first stage is to predict the touching points of the inner and outer channels by carrying forward the same spacing of touching points as in the previous price history. These are marked by the arrows at the predicted outer channel boundary. The inner channel is then drawn, keeping a constant depth and aiming to touch the outer boundary at the indicated touching points

Since the depth of this projected inner channel is about 35 divisions, and at this point we do not know where the future data will lie at any particular time, except that it should lie within the channel, we are able to predict a future data point to within 35 divisions. Since the vertical scale of these diagrams runs from zero up to 180, an accuracy of 35 divisions means, in percentage terms, a prediction accuracy to within 20% for any future data point. To some of you, this might sound astonishing, and to others it might sound rather disappointing, depending on your perspective. To put it into context, however, most investors would be unable to predict a share price one year ahead to better than 50%. Even more importantly, the 20% accuracy has nothing to do with the accuracy or otherwise of the channel analysis method. It is due to the fact that there is a 20% random, i.e. unpredictable, content in the original complex data. Putting it another way, we are able to predict the predictable, i.e. non-random, part of the complex movement with almost 100% accuracy! The accuracy of this prediction is shown graphically in Figure 5.9. The inner channel we established in Figure 5.8 is shown superimposed on the actual data, which have been taken from Figure 4.21 in the last chapter. It can be seen that the data do stay fairly closely within the boundaries of the predicted inner channel.

This prediction of future share price movement has been carried out by using two channels, and we have seen that these two channels have been sufficient for us to be able to determine the wavelengths and amplitudes of two cycles present in the data as well as the amplitude of the random movement. In stock market data there will usually be many more than two cycles present, and we will have to draw more outer channels in order to be able to carry out a full analysis, although there will be occasions where we are only interested in one or two cycles. In such a case the above procedure will be sufficient. Where we do need to analyse for more cycles, we have to use exactly the same deductive methods above in order to determine the touching points of each channel with the next outer channel. Having determined these touching points, we must start with the projection of the outermost channel into the future and indicate the predicted touching points of the next inner channel on it. We can then extrapolate this next inner channel so as to touch the outer at these points. We then move in a level and indicate the touching points of the next inner channel and carry out the same procedure. We keep doing this until we run out of channels.

The important message from this exercise, therefore, is that channel analysis is an extremely powerful technique for the prediction of share price movement, being able to predict with great accuracy the future position of the various cycles which are present in the share price data. In predicting the actual share price at some time in the future, it will be most successful for those shares in which the random price movement is lowest. It will also be most successful in predicting the near future rather than the distant future, since small inaccuracies in the graphical projections will become magnified the further away from the present time we move.

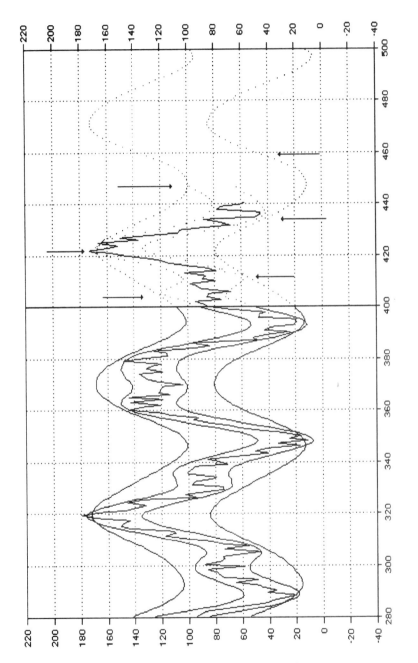

Figure 5.9 The plot of the actual data after week 400 stays quite closely to the predicted inner channel

6

The Cycles Present in Share Price Data

In the last chapter we showed that any cyclical waveform is defined totally by three quantities—its wavelength, its amplitude and its position in time. We also showed that complex data in which two different cycles were superimposed on random movement could be analysed by the use of moving averages or graphical channel analysis so that future movement of the data could be predicted with an accuracy that depended upon the amount of random movement present. This leads to the conclusion that for such analyses to be of any use in predicting the behaviour of share prices, the following should be an essential prerequisite:

- The amount of random movement should be relatively small.
- The number of different cycles present should also be small.
- These cyclic components should be present to a greater or lesser degree in all share price movement.

We said in the last chapter that we could do nothing about predicting random price movement, since by definition, random movement is unpredictable movement. If 50% of a share price movement is random, then the best that we can achieve is to predict the other 50% non-random movement. If random movement accounts for less than 10% of the share price movement, then we are in the fortunate position of being able to predict, at least theoretically, over 90% of the future price movement.

Fortunately for us, the majority of share price movement is non-random, although the proportion varies from one share to another and from one time period to another in the history of any one share. Therefore, we do have the possibility of achieving good price predictions over the short term.

If the great proportion of price movement is not random, then it is important that the number of cyclic components present is not large, otherwise the analysis reaches such a level of complexity that powerful computers are necessary to wade through all the mathematics necessary to resolve these. Again, fortunately, the number of important cycles which can be discerned in share price data amount to just a handful, and these are present to a greater or lesser degree in all share prices. This means that each share price can be treated somewhat similarly, and reduces the amount of work which would have to be done if all share prices were completely different. This fortunate combination of circumstances makes it possible for us to apply the techniques we used in the last chapter with a high probability of success.

Work carried out by a number of analysts this century has led to the conclusion that the main cycles which can be identified in share price data are those shown in Table 6.1. As far as the amplitude of the cycles is concerned, this appears to be directly proportional to the wavelength of the cycle until we get up to cycles of wavelength longer than 4.3 years. The amplitude then increases more slowly than this direct relationship. Thus the amplitude of the 4.3-year cycle is about 1.34 times that of the 3.2-year cycle (4.3/3.2 = 1.34), but the amplitude of the 9.2-year cycle is only 1.67 times that of the 4.3-year cycle and not the 2.13 times it would be if the increase was directly proportional to the wavelength. Likewise, the amplitude of the 16-year cycle is about 2.10 times that of the 4.3-year cycle and not the 3.72 times we might have expected.

These amplitudes, of course, rank the cycles in order of their importance in their effect on the share price, since obviously the 4.3-year cycle moves the price over 50 times more than does the 4-week cycle. This ranking of the amplitudes has to be tempered by the practical aspects of the needs of the investor. It is no good telling him that the 36-year cycle has just passed its peak and that he should not invest for another 18 years when the cycle starts to rise again! To all intents and purposes the investor has to concern himself with cycles of 4.3 years and lower wavelengths. As we shall see, the

Table 6.1 Known cycles in share price data

Years	Months	Weeks	Days (business)*	Relative amplitude
54				150
36				132
16				117.1
9.5				95.8
9.2				93.1
7.1				82.5
4.3	51	223		55.75
3.2	38	166		41.5
1.8	21	94		23.5
0.8	9.6	42		10.5
		33	165	8.25
		9	45	2.25
		7	35	1.75
		4	20	1

*Five business days in a week.

investor still makes a considerable profit if he can judge the turning point
of a shorter duration cycle even if a longer term one is headed downwards.
The best moves in the share price are made when several cycles have
arrived at their troughs, and the upward movement in all of them occurring at nearly the same time will be additive in effect, as we noticed for the
simple examples in Chapter 4.

So far we have given the impression that the cycles present in share
prices are permanent, and that all of the uncertainty in movement is due to
random movement. However, we now have to draw attention to another
fact, and that is that the cycles themselves are subject to variation. The
variation occurs in two dimensions—in the wavelength and in the amplitude. The variation in wavelength usually amounts to a small percentage
of the actual wavelength. In real terms it means that we have to predict a
"window of time" for the occurrence of a future peak or trough rather
than an exact point in time. Taking the 42-week cycle in share prices as an
example, the next peak could occur at any point from say 40 weeks to 44
weeks onwards from the previous peak. A difference of more than 10%
before or after the expected position for a peak would be unusual.

The use of a time window in the analysis of a share price does not cause
any difficulty, since the investor will start to expect a cycle to turn upwards
or downwards at the beginning of the window, and will not be unduly
perturbed when the turn does not come instantly. The important point is
that he is expecting it to occur and will recognise its occurrence when it
happens, even though it is later than expected. The effect of this variation
in wavelength and the use of a time window is illustrated in Figure 6.1.

The effect of variation in amplitude means that a peak or trough may
occur at a higher or lower point on the price scale than expected by
comparison with a previous peak or trough. In other words a peak or
trough can undershoot or overshoot the predicted price level. This effect is
illustrated in Figure 6.2.

The variation in amplitude can be so severe that a cycle can cease to
exist at a certain point in time, reappearing much later and building up in
amplitude. The fortunate aspect of this variation in amplitude is that the
change is not abrupt but gradual in nature. Amplitude can slowly decrease
over a period of say five or six complete wavelengths and then begin to
increase slowly back to somewhere near the maximum amplitude. Another way of looking at this is to say that the amplitude exhibits its own
cyclicality. This change in amplitude is one reason why it is not sensible to
predict too far ahead. The amplitude five complete wavelengths into the
future is much less predictable than the amplitude just one wavelength
into the future. As with the variation in wavelength, amplitude variation is
such that a peak or trough is normally no more than 10% above or below
the point which the last peak or trough reached on the price scale.

Since we have now established that there is a horizontal uncertainty in a
peak or trough position (i.e. in wavelength) and a vertical uncertainty (i.e.

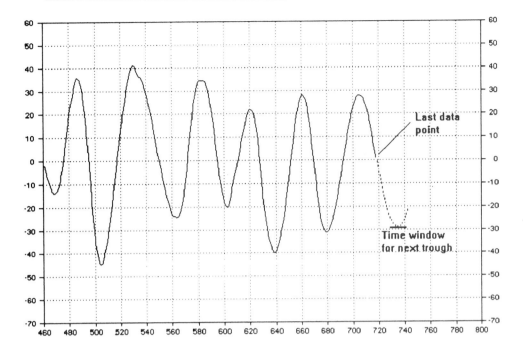

Figure 6.1 Wavelength variation—how a time window has to be applied to take care of the uncertainty in the prediction of when a trough will occur

in amplitude) then these two uncertainties combine to form a rectangular "prediction box". The exact centre of the box is the predicted point at which the peak or trough should occur in time and in amplitude, and obviously the dimensions of the box reflect the uncertainty. The more certain we are about the prediction point, the smaller the box, while conversely if we are rather uncertain, then the box will be larger. The concept of a prediction box is illustrated in Figure 6.3.

Since the box has finite dimensions, a share price can spend some time in it before making the predicted move upwards or downwards. It is not correct to make our investment or disinvestment at the moment the box is entered, because we may find that the share price hovers at about the same level for a number of weeks. We might also find that temporary random forces are such as to negate the movement completely so that the anticipated move does not occur. Because of this it is necessary to devise techniques to apply to the share price once the box has been entered in order to decide the optimum moment to take action or to decide that the optimum moment may not arrive at all. This approach can only be illustrated later when real examples are discussed.

Having spent some time in the analysis of artificially generated complex waveforms, it is now time to apply the techniques to a share price history.

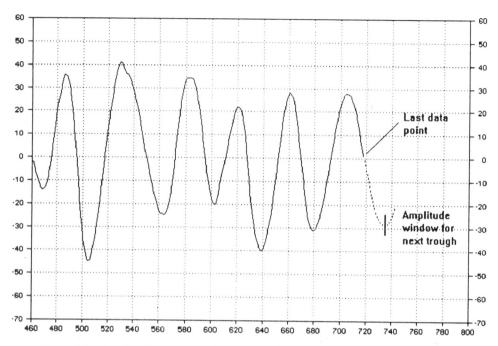

Figure 6.2 Amplitude variation—how an amplitude window has to be applied to take care of the uncertainty in the prediction of the depth of a future trough

AN ANALYSIS OF THE REDLAND SHARE PRICE

The share price history of Redland is shown in Figure 6.4. A number of cycles can be observed quite easily. Note that even the sharp fall during the crash of 1987 was followed by an equally sharp rise.

Random and Very Short Term Movement

The analysis should start by answering the question about the degree of random content in the movement of the Redland share price. The week-to-week random movement is rather difficult to unravel from very short wavelengths of a few weeks' duration, but we can start by isolating the combination of these two. In previous chapters we showed that very short term and random movement could be removed by using a moving average of short span, or highlighted by calculating a short span moving average difference. As a start, a span of say nine weeks would be useful in separating out all movement of nine weeks and less periodicity, including random movement, from the longer term cycles which sweep the price up and down by quite large amounts. The nine-week average difference is shown in Figure 6.5.

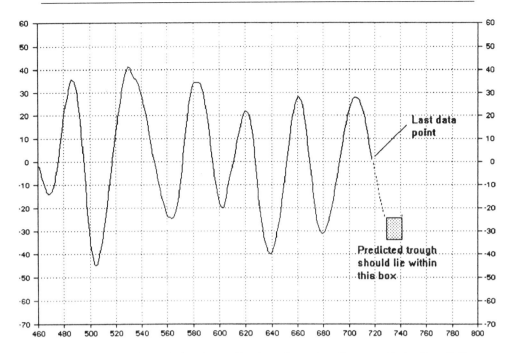

Figure 6.3 How the variation in amplitude and wavelength means that a "prediction box" must be drawn for the estimated position of a future trough

Note that most of the time, this random/short term movement only swings between the –20 and +20 points on the vertical price scale. This means that 40p of the price movement of Redland shares is accounted for by random week-to-week movement and cyclical movement of 10 weeks' or less wavelength. Since the Redland share price ranged from a low of approximately 250p to a high of 650p in the chart, i.e. a change of 400p, taking the whole period from the beginning of 1982, then most of the time the random and short term cyclical fluctuations account for about 10% of the total price movement. This very important and surprising fact can be expressed in another way: taken on average over an eight-year period, about 90% of the Redland share price movement is due to a combination of cyclical movements of greater than nine weeks' periodicity. Since we have learned how to isolate the various cycles which may be present in complex data, then we appear to have the key to predicting the future Redland share price!

This exciting prospect has to be tempered somewhat by rather more consideration of the nature of the random or unexpected movement. We pointed out that the random movement and short term movement was about 10% over a 14-year period, in other words it averaged this over a long time. Unfortunately, an average value derived from a large number of values can contain a few extreme values. A closer look at Figure 6.5 shows

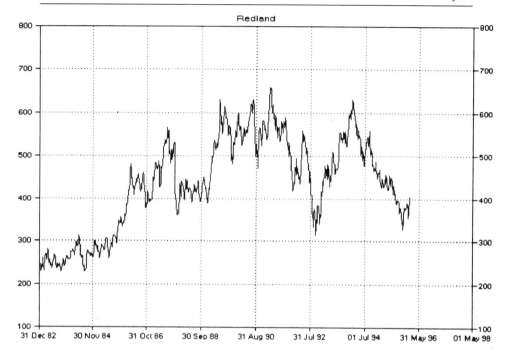

Figure 6.4   The share price of Redland since the beginning of 1983

that the random or short term movement did reach much more extreme values than 10% on about a dozen occasions over the 14-year period. On two of the occasions they accounted for swings of about 80p in the share price. Of course, we do not particularly care whether we call these swings random or short term movement. The fact is that their amplitudes were much larger than expected and they came out of the blue. Any price predictions made just prior to their occurrence would therefore have been considerably in error.

This fact has to be clearly understood—most of the time the random and short term fluctuations will amount to only about 40p of any price movement, and this is the tolerance we will have to put on predicted price movement. The probability is therefore that our predictions will be good, but about one in every 20 predictions will experience this unexpectedly large rise or fall. Since in the case of Redland there were 12 occasions of such a large swing in 14 years, the average time elapsed between such swings is just over one year. The longest length of time without such a large unexpected rise or fall was nearly 200 weeks, and the shortest about 20 weeks. From this we can come to a conclusion that it is unlikely that such a large unexpected effect will occur within 20 weeks of the last such occurrence. We can therefore see that our predictions at points in time a few weeks after such a large swing should be much more accurate than

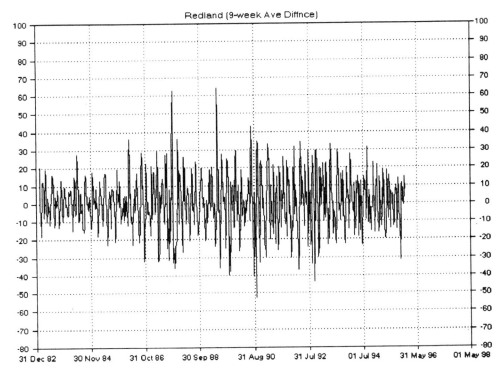

Figure 6.5 The nine-week moving average difference of the Redland share price. This shows random movement and any cyclical movement of nine weeks' or less periodicity. Note that the majority of the movement lies between –20 and +20p, i.e. is less than 40p on the vertical price scale

those which may be made when a swing of this nature has not occurred for a long time. If we predict only a short period ahead we are less likely to be caught by the unexpected than if we try to predict say for six months or a full year ahead of the present time.

Movement of Less Than 53-Week Periodicity

Since the method of looking at random and very short term movements in Redland was successful in showing that about 10% of the price movement fell into this category, it is useful to look at longer term fluctuations. In Figure 6.6 is shown the 53-week average difference of the Redland share price. This shows up random movement plus any cycles of less than one year's periodicity.

The response shown in Figure 6.6 also includes all of the movement shown in Figure 6.5. We can see that most of the movement fell between –60p and +60p, i.e. 120p on the vertical scale. On about 12 occasions the movement fell outside these limits. Thus we can see that the fluctuations of

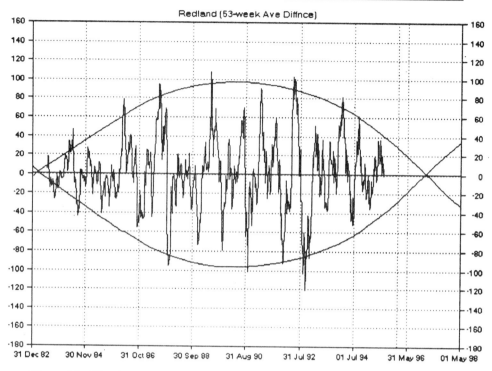

Figure 6.6 The 53-week moving average difference of the Redland share price shows random movement plus cyclical movement of less than one year's periodicity. The amplitude is varying in a long term cyclical fashion as shown by the boundaries

less than one year's periodicity therefore accounted for about 30% of the overall price range of 400p.

It is interesting to see the gradual change in amplitude of these short term cycles over the 14-year period covered by the data. In Figure 6.6 an envelope is drawn around these fluctuations in order to highlight the regular nature of the change. The combined amplitude passes through a maximum between 1989 and 1992, and at the time of writing is at a level similar to that seen in 1983.

Movement of Less than 103-Week Periodicity

Using a 103-week average difference, the chart shown in Figure 6.7 is produced. Now, most of the movement lies between –80p and +80p, with a few larger movements running from –140p to +120p. Thus these fluctuations of less than two years' periodicity account for 160p, or about 40% of the overall price movement.

This is about as far as it is possible to go in looking at the contributions of wide categories of cycle periodicities to the share price, but it has been a very constructive exercise.

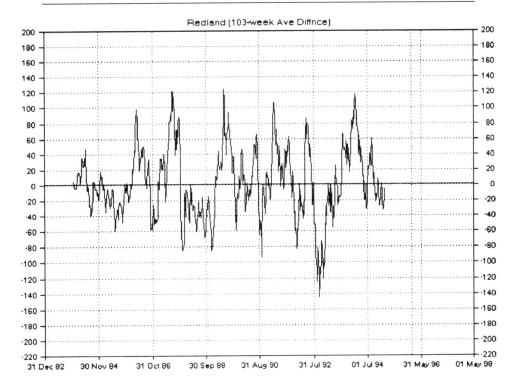

Figure 6.7 The 103-week moving average difference of the Redland share price shows random movement plus cyclical movement of less than two years' periodicity

Selected Cycles in Redland Price Data

By using the cycle highlighter which was discussed in Chapter 4, information about the current and near-future status of selected cycles can be obtained. By using a selection of such cycles, it is possible to come to a conclusion about the most likely direction of the share price over the near future. Since the previous exercise showed us that 30% of the price movement could be attributed to cycles of less than two years' periodicity, then the status of the one-year, six-month and three-month cycles will be useful.

The 53-week cycle, plus the share price data, is shown in Figure 6.8. The data end on 2nd February 1996. It can be seen that the cycle has passed its low point and is now rising. The low point in the cycle was on 24th November 1995, and the next predicted high point, half a span, i.e. 27 weeks, into the future, will be on 31st May 1996. From the current point of 2nd February we can therefore expect 17 weeks of rise before the peak is reached. Its low point on 24th November corresponds also to a point in time somewhere between the two recent low points in the share price of

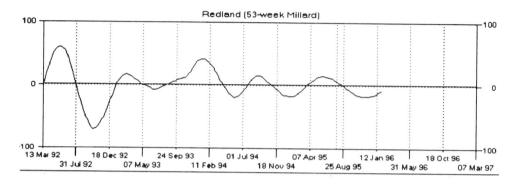

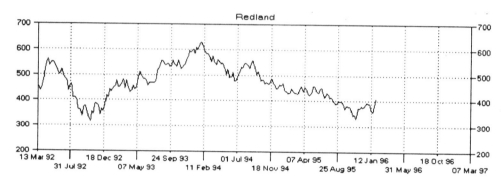

Figure 6.8   The 53-week cycle in Redland isolated by means of the cycle highlighter

345p and 375p. The amplitude of the cycle has decreased considerably from the value of about 120p in 1992, and is now accounting for about 40p of price movement. At the current price level of 400p, this means that a correct interpretation of its low point would give the investor a probable 40p, i.e. 10%, price rise even if other favourable cycles are ignored. Since we are now just past the low, we would anticipate that this cycle should contribute a rise of about 30p to the share price over the next 17 weeks.

Moving to shorter term cycles, the 27-week cycle is shown in Figure 6.9. This can be seen to be falling at the time of the latest data point, 2nd February 1996. The last peak was at 15th December 1995, so the next low would be half a span, i.e. 13 weeks, on from this point. This takes us to 22nd March 1996. Since the latest data point is on 2nd February 1996, we expect a further seven weeks of fall before the next trough is reached. It can be seen that the latest point of the cycle is below the zero level, so we expect this cycle to contribute a fall of about 15p over the next seven weeks.

The 13-week cycle is shown in Figure 6.10. The last high point in the cycle was on 22nd December 1995, and the next low point would be half a

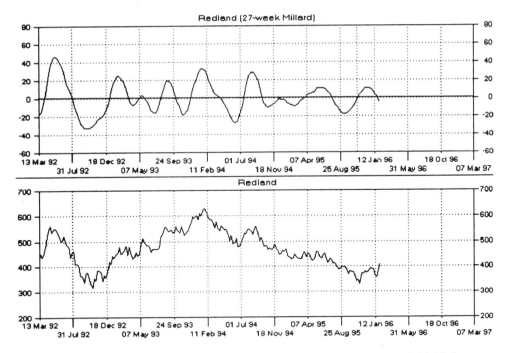

Figure 6.9 The 27-week cycle in Redland isolated by means of the cycle highlighter

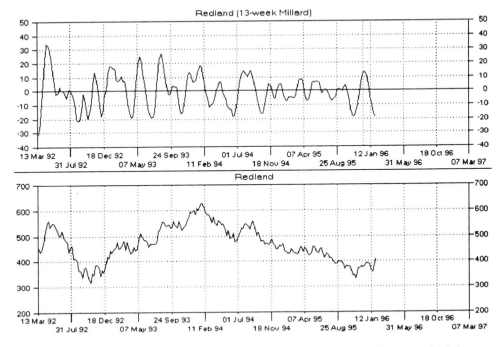

Figure 6.10 The 13-week cycle in Redland isolated by means of the cycle highlighter

span, i.e. seven weeks, further on in time. This takes us to 9th February 1996, i.e. one week into the future from the latest data point. The amplitude of the cycle is about 30p, so, following a further small fall the following week, it is expected to add some 30p to the share price over the subsequent seven weeks.

At this point we have a great deal of information about cycles in Redland of 53 weeks' or less periodicity. Before using these data to predict the future price behaviour in Redland it is important to have a view of longer term cycles. Cycles of longer than 53 weeks' wavelength will be isolated by using a moving average of more than 53 weeks. A 103-week span would be a sensible value to select, since cycles of longer than two years would be highlighted by applying this span. The 103-week average together with the price data is shown in Figure 6.11.

It can be seen that this average, which terminates half a span, i.e. one year, in the past, was still falling at its last calculated point. The problem is to estimate what it is doing at the present time. The last high point in the average was at 14th February 1994, while the previous low point was on 9th October 1992. These are 66 weeks apart in time. If the composite waveform which is being isolated by this average is symmetrical, then it would have reached a low point 66 weeks on from 14th February 1994, i.e. on 21st April 1995, about ten months prior to the latest data point on 2nd February 1996. Quite obviously, we are in a situation where, if this long term cycle has not turned up, then the turnaround is greatly overdue. Thus there is a very high probability that the long term trend has bottomed out or is about to bottom out. If the long term trend bottomed out exactly on 21st April 1995, i.e. was perfectly symmetrical, then we would therefore expect a rise which would last for at least 66 weeks on from 21st April 1995, i.e. until 26th July 1996. This is still some 25 weeks away from the latest point on 2nd February 1996. If the cycle bottomed out later than this, or has yet to bottom out, then the long term trend will peak even later in the future. Thus, at the very minimum we can expect nearly six months of a rising long term trend. Since the latest amplitude of this cycle is about 100p, this upward trend should add that amount to the share price. This amplitude is spread over a nominal 66 weeks, i.e. contributes about 1.5p per week to the share price rise.

Now is the time to list all of the facts we have obtained by this analysis of cycles in order to be able to make a prediction for the future:

- 13-week cycle: will rise over the next seven weeks, adding 30p to the share price at the rate of just over 4p per week.
- 27-week cycle: will fall over the next seven weeks, taking some 15p off the share price at the rate of about 2p per week.

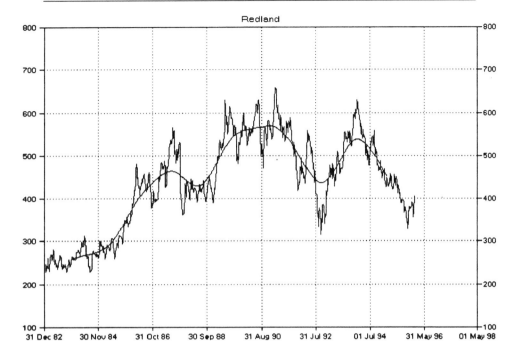

Figure 6.11 The centred 103-week average of the Redland share price is superimposed on the price data. Long term cycles are very obvious

- 53-week cycle: will rise over the next 17 weeks with an anticipated contribution of 30p to the share price at the rate of about 0.75p per week.
- Longer wavelengths: the sum of all these has probably already started to rise. The amplitude of about 100p means that this will cause a rise of about 1.5p per week.

Short Term Prediction from the Data

How far ahead we can predict in the short term depends upon the value of the shortest wavelength that we have extracted. In the above case we extracted a 13-week cycle, which means that the peak-to-peak distance is 13 weeks, while the trough-to-peak distance is six or seven weeks. Bearing in mind the comments at the beginning of this chapter on wavelength and amplitude variation, it is dangerous to predict further ahead than half of a wavelength, and preferably even less than this. Thus, with a 13-week cycle as the shortest cycle in the data, a prediction of the situation about five weeks ahead is about optimum.

Thus, over the next five weeks:

- The 13-week cycle will add 5 × 4p = 20p
- The 27-week cycle will remove 5 × 2p = –10p
- The 53-week cycle will add 5 × 0.75p = 3.75p
- The long term cycle might add 5 × 1.5p = 7.5p

Note that the position of the long term cycle has been estimated. Although it might be rising, it might also be just approaching its low point. If the latter, the negative contribution will be quite small, since the nearer the peak or trough, the smaller is the weekly change in its contribution.

Thus the net effect of all of these contributions is for a rise over the next few weeks, probably of about 20p. There will also be day-to-day random movement occurring, which may be additive, or may be subtractive. Thus we should put a range on the anticipated rise as being between say 10p and 30p, but at least we can predict a rise rather than a fall.

The actual progression of the share price from its value of 404p on 2nd February was: 9th February, 412p; 16th February, 418p; 23rd February, 417p; 1st March, 435p; 8th March, 419p. Thus the actual rise was 31p, very close to the top end of the predicted range. This shows the power of this method of extracting cycles in order to predict a short term change in share price, with the proviso that the short term is less than half of the value of the shortest wavelength that has been extracted. Investors in traded options will immediately see the value of such short-term predictions.

Longer Term Prediction from the Data

Since the longest term cycle isolated from the 103-week average is predicted to top out on 26th July 1996 at the soonest, we can make a prediction about the share price on 26th July 1996, i.e. over five months into the future. We will have to estimate at what point each of the shorter term cycles will be in their development by that point in the future, subject to the comments on variation in wavelength and amplitude. We can now start to see the value of predicting the long term cycle, since by 26th July it will have added about 40p to the current value (404p) of the share price on 2nd February. Thus the relative importance of the short term cycles in the overall picture is diminishing rapidly, so that the uncertainty in their position is much less important than when a short term prediction is made and the long term cycle makes very little contribution.

If, for the purposes of making some kind of prediction, we assume the short term cycles to behave completely regularly, then by 26th July 1996 their status will be as follows:

- 13-week cycle: will bottom out in about two weeks
- 27-week cycle: nearly halfway down to its low point

- 53-week cycle: about one-third of the way down to its low point
- Longer wavelengths: probably at the top or nearly so

In order to predict, we will have to take the change in contribution from what it was on 2nd February to what it is estimated to be on 26th July.

The 13-week cycle is at about the same position, so there will be no net contribution from this. The 27-week cycle is also at about the same position, so there will be no net contribution from this. The 53-week cycle was about one-third of the way up from the bottom on 2nd February, whereas it is predicted to be one-third of the way down on 26th July. The difference in contribution is therefore about one-third of the amplitude, one-third of 40p, or 13p higher than it was on 2nd February.

Thus the net effect of these cycles is to add 13p to the price of 404p, while the long term cycle will add perhaps 40p to the price, giving an estimated price on 26th July of 457p.

The share price movement of Redland up to the end of September 1996 is shown in Figure 6.12. While the price was at 415p on 26th July, i.e. only 11p higher than on 2nd February, it then moved up rapidly to reach the estimated level of 456p on 23rd August 1996. Thus our prediction, while correct in actual price, was about one month premature in the timing. Bearing in mind that our estimation of the position of the long term cycles was based on the

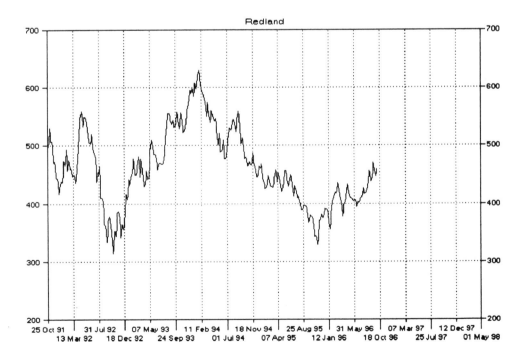

Figure 6.12 The share price of Redland up to the end of September 1996

fact that the long term cycle had probably bottomed out, this is an excellent achievement from first principles, and shows the value of a structured approach to price prediction using cycles in the share price data.

Prediction Using Channel Analysis

It is now of interest to carry out a prediction of the Redland share price based on the channel analysis method which was applied to artificial data in Chapters 4 and 5 to see if it is consistent with the results obtained purely from the application of cycle analysis.

Figure 6.13 shows a channel drawn around the Redland share price. The first impression from the chart is that the channel is currently falling, but that the price possibly bounced up from the bottom boundary of the channel in November 1995 when it reached 328p.

Since the price is rapidly approaching the upper boundary, the first deduction from this chart is that we expect the price to rebound downwards again, so that the investor should stay clear.

The date of 2nd February 1996 was deliberately chosen so as to be just after a channel turning point, when in fact the price started to rise. In order to deduce this from channel analysis it is essential to draw a longer term channel in order to demonstrate that the first impression of a falling channel is inaccurate.

This outer channel is shown in Figure 6.14. The critical points which determine its position are the series of major highs between 1989 and 1990, the major low in August 1992 and the most recent major low in November 1995. In order to keep a constant depth and avoid extreme rates of curvature in this outer channel, it has to be drawn so that it is virtually horizontal at the latest point in time, i.e. on 2nd February 1996. By the rules of channel analysis, we cannot allow inner channels to cross an outer channel by more than a small amount. Thus we have to draw the inner channel so as to bounce upwards from the lower boundary of the outer channel. This puts a totally different complexion on the prediction of the future share price from that which followed the drawing of just one channel. We now interpret the current long term trend as rising, and since the shorter term channel containing the price movement is contained within it, the outlook is for a rise in the share price. If we conclude that the outer channel is likely to remain horizontal for some time, then we have a target area for the share price as being near the upper boundary of the outer channel, which will be at about 625p.

We note also that the inner channel has developed a much more obvious cyclicality than was present in the early part of the chart. This is important, because such cyclicality normally persists for at least one and a half complete cycles, i.e. one and a half wavelengths. By this is meant that the amplitude remains important for this length of time. It should be mentioned once again that the amplitude is subject to change over a period of

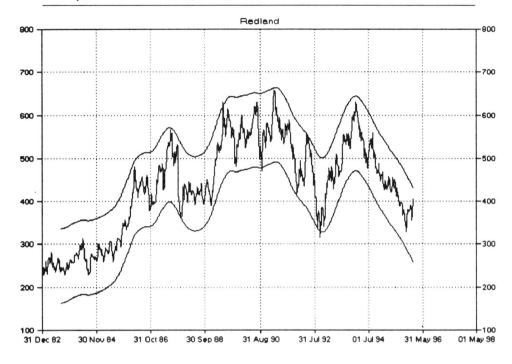

Figure 6.13 A channel drawn around the Redland share price movement as at 2nd February 1996

time, and the wavelength will also change from its nominal value. More examples of this will be seen later.

That the nominal wavelength is changing can be determined by looking at the latest succession of peaks and troughs, a wavelength being of course twice the distance between a trough and the following peak, or a peak and the following trough. The major low (313p) on 16th October 1992 was at week 511 from the beginning of the chart, the next high (630p) was on 28th January 1994 at week 578, and the latest low (328p) on 10th November 1995 at week 671. Thus on 28th January 1994 the wavelength of this important cycle was $2 \times (578 - 511) = 134$ weeks. On 10th November 1995 the wavelength was $2 \times (671 - 578) = 186$ weeks. We can see therefore that the wavelength is increasing. What cannot be determined is whether it has reached a maximum value and will start to decrease again, or whether it will continue to increase. Since we have two such possibilities, the easiest way forward for the moment is to assume that the wavelength will remain the same. This means that the next peak will be half a wavelength, i.e. 93 weeks, on from the last trough which was at week 671. This now gives us a rough idea of the most likely point in time when the price will arrive at the top of the channel. It will be on week $671 + 93$, i.e. week 764. This corresponds to 22nd August 1997. Since we know that the wavelength and

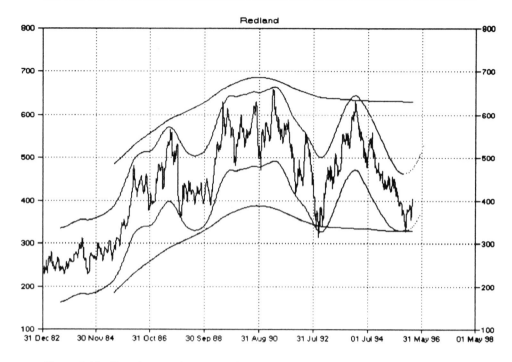

Figure 6.14 Drawing another outer channel aids in the prediction of price movement by showing where the inner channel must reverse direction

amplitude are unlikely to remain the same, all we need to do now is to put a time window and price window on this prediction. This is our "prediction box" (Figure 6.15), and it is extremely useful as the target area into which we expect the price to move.

We can see that by comparing the method of moving average/cycle analysis and channel analysis, we get broadly similar conclusions for the progress of the Redland share price in the near future.

APPLYING CHANNEL ANALYSIS TO THE BUYING AND SELLING OF BAA SHARES

The power of channel analysis is fully illustrated by showing how an investor would have decided when to buy and sell BAA shares at various points over the last five years. Even using weekly data, a surprising insight into the behaviour of the share price will be obtained, and we shall start with this before moving to a discussion of the even better results that can be obtained using daily data. We can start the analysis by putting ourselves in the position of an investor monitoring the BAA share price from July 1993 onwards.

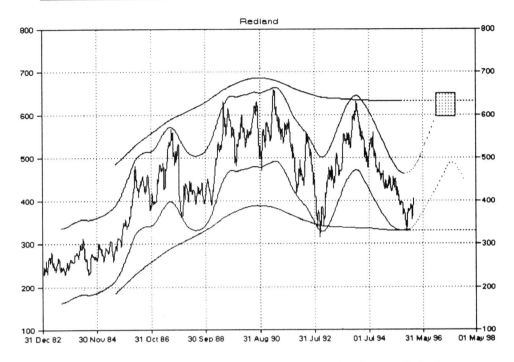

Figure 6.15 Based on the wavelength of the inner channel cycle, a prediction box can be drawn around 22nd August 1997 as the target area for the future price rise

July 1993 (Figure 6.16)

The channels which could be drawn for the BAA share price data during July 1993 are shown in Figure 6.16. The peaks which partly define the upper boundary are those in July 1990, June 1992, December 1992 and March 1993. Since there are no major peaks in the share price between July 1990 and June 1992, it would not be possible to draw one obvious upper boundary but rather a series of curves of differing concavity when viewed from the top of the chart.

Fortunately, there are troughs which partly define the lower boundary in this empty region, and since the boundaries have to be at a constant vertical distance apart, the combination of upper peaks and lower troughs enables us to draw just one channel, as is shown in Figure 6.16.

When the more minor peaks and troughs are taken into account, and maintaining the constant depth criterion, an inner channel can also be drawn in a similar manner. In this case the inner channel touches the outer channel at the positions of the peaks and troughs which were used to define the outer channel.

The depth of the outer channel is equivalent to about 65p on the price scale, while the inner channel has a depth of about 30p. On 7th May, the

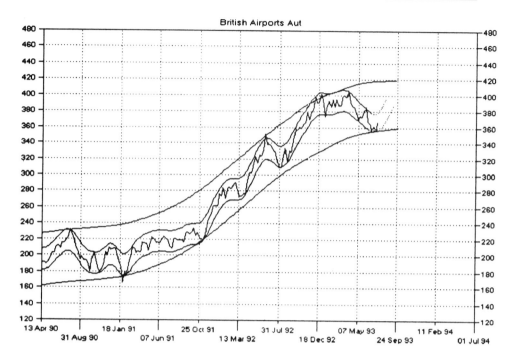

Figure 6.16 Channel analysis of the BAA share price in July 1993 from weekly data

price, at 369.5p, is somewhere around the mid-point of the outer channel, and at the lower boundary of the inner channel, which is falling within the outer channel. We thus expect the price to bounce upwards from the lower boundary of the inner channel, but the price rise to be limited by the fact that this channel is falling. This is indeed what happened, since the price rose over the next few weeks to 382.5p by 4th June, before falling again to a low of 356.5p on 25th June. It rose the next week to 361.5p before falling back again to 356.5p on 9th July. It rose from this point to 365.5p on 16th July, thus confirming that the previous week was indeed a trough in the price. It is at this point that we are trying to decide on the future price movement of the share.

Attention now turns to the outer channel. We are confident that it is running almost horizontally at this point by virtue of the fact that the group of peaks in December 1992 and March 1993 are at a similar level. The price at 356.5p is just about at the lower boundary, but we can also deduce that the falling inner channel has now reached its lowest point because the two troughs on 25th June and 9th July are at the same level, and these almost certainly lie on the boundary.

Taking the position that the outer channel is running horizontally, the inner channel has stopped falling and the share price itself is at both of these lower boundaries, then the share now appears to be a good buy at 365.5p.

That this decision was correct is confirmed by the subsequent rise in price to 535.5p by 7th September 1993. Thus a rise of 170p, or 46%, was captured by using the logic of channel analysis.

February 1994 (Figure 6.17)

By this point in time, the inner channel is clearly rising, and the outer channel, which was horizontal in the previous example, is now rising again. We are at the point where the inner channel is at, or very close to, the most likely position of the upper boundary of the outer channel. Thus we expect the inner channel to bounce back again, and this extrapolated future course for the inner channel has been drawn in Figure 6.17.

In such a position, the price movement has to be watched very carefully. Just as in the previous example a succession of two troughs at just about the same level indicated that the inner channel had stopped falling, then so does the succession of two peaks where the second is at the same or a lower level than the first indicate that the inner channel has stopped rising. In the present case, the peak at 535.5p on 7th January was followed by a fall to 522.5p and then eventually a rise to 532.5p on 4th February. It was not until the following week when the price fell to 519p that the price the previous week was seen to be a peak.

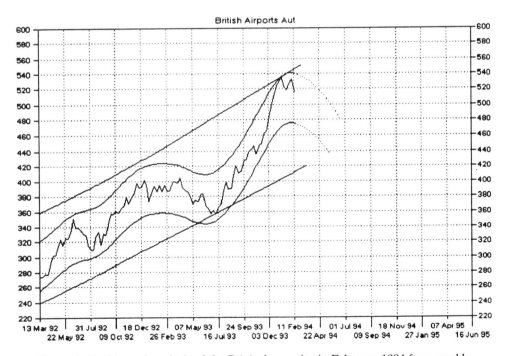

Figure 6.17 Channel analysis of the BAA share price in February 1994 from weekly data

Thus on 11th February we are in a position to take a decision. The failure of the second peak to rise above the first one indicates quite strongly that the inner channel has topped out and has just started on its way down. Thus the share has to be sold at this value of 519p. As a result, the real gain from the investment made on 16th July at 365.5p is 153.5p, or 42% in about six months.

July/August 1994 (Figure 6.18)

By May 1994, the outer channel still appears to be rising, but the fall in price to 455p by 25th May would mean that the lower boundary is being penetrated. In order to avoid this the channel will have to be made to gradually flatten out from the point where the peak in January 1994 is at the upper boundary. This is shown in Figure 6.18.

The price rises from 455p over the next two weeks to 475p, but then drops again. As the price drops to a new low point at 441p on 24th June, the channel has to be bent even further to accommodate this point as being on the boundary. We are hoping for a rise so that this point at 441p becomes a trough lying on the lower boundary. This trough is indeed formed by the rise the following week to 446p. We are now in the

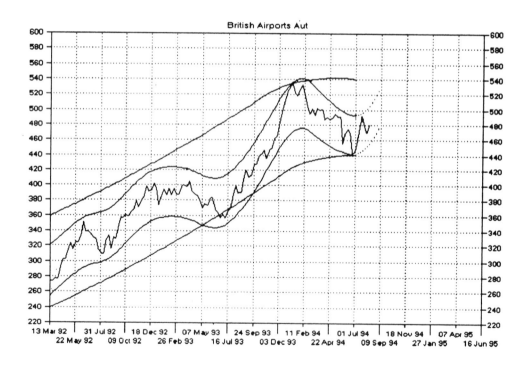

Figure 6.18 Channel analysis of the BAA share price in July 1994 from weekly data

situation where the outer channel has virtually topped out, and is running horizontally, and the price has risen from a trough which is exactly on the boundary. This estimated position of the outer channel imposes a bounce on the inner channel. Thus all depends upon our estimation of the outer channel. If it is correct, then the bounce in the inner channel will take the price up with it towards the upper boundary of the outer channel. We now need to wait for the next minor trough to be formed at a higher level than 441p in order to confirm that short term trends have now turned up and will take the price upwards. If the next trough is lower than 441p, then we will be forced to bend the outer channel again to accommodate it. The bend required would thus cause the outer channel to fall.

Obviously the best time for investment is when the outer channel is rising, but profits can also be made when a channel is flattening out. The time to avoid investment is when the outer channel is falling, since by the time the price reaches the upper boundary it may well be at a lower level than when it started. These comparisons are shown at the end of this chapter. In the present case, therefore, if the next trough is lower than 441p then we would leave the share alone.

The price rose for the next four weeks to 488p before falling back to 476.5p and then rising again. Thus, indeed, the trough now formed is considerably higher than the previous one at 441p, so that we can be sure that the share price is in a short term upward trend. The trouble is that when the outer channel is running horizontally, the upper boundary is at about 540p. Thus from the current level of 480p in August 1994 we have a somewhat restricted potential for gain of only about 12.5%. In such a case it would be unwise to make an investment.

The analysis of the position in August 1994 has been extremely useful. If the second trough had been formed quickly after the first one at 441p, and at a level only slightly higher, then the investment would have had a greater profit potential. As it is, the fact that the trough was formed 35p higher removed much of the potential profit, making it unattractive. As we shall see in the next section, using daily data will often clarify the position in such cases.

THE ADVANTAGE OF DAILY DATA

These excellent results using weekly closing prices would satisfy most investors, but it should be obvious that even better results will be obtained using daily data. This is because lower prices may be reached before the end of a week, giving a better buying opportunity. The same argument applies to selling where a better price might be achieved. Not only that, but warning signals that the price is about to reverse will be much more accurate, so that trouble can be avoided much sooner.

July 1993 (Figure 6.19)

The daily data for BAA from the high point in March 1993 to July 1993 are shown in Figure 6.19. In the earlier discussion of the channels which could be drawn using weekly data we came to the conclusion that the outer channel was running horizontally because of the fact that the groups of peaks in December 1992 and March 1993 were at a similar level. The daily chart shows that the peak in December 1992 was higher than the set of peaks in March 1993. From this we can conclude that the outer channel has turned slightly downwards, but not at such a rate as to negate the possibility of an investment when the price reaches the lower boundary.

As far as the inner channel is concerned, the first major trough, at 356.5p on 25th June, lies on the lower boundary. However, the next trough at 354.5p on 12th July is at a higher level than would be the case with the slope of the inner channel being maintained. We can conclude that the inner channel may be about to change direction, especially as it is rapidly approaching the extrapolated position of the lower boundary. We now have to wait for the next trough to be formed, which we hope will lie at a higher level than 354.5p in order to confirm the change of direction. After rising from 354.5p for seven days, the price falls to 361p, and then rises the next day to 368p. We now have our trough, and it is indeed at a higher

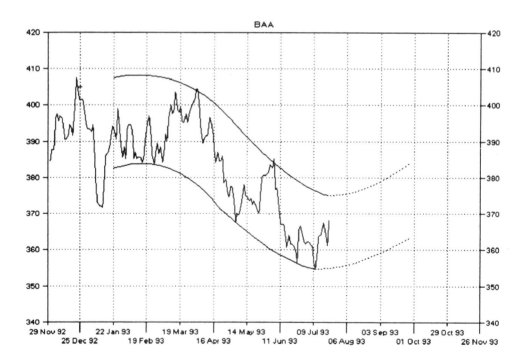

Figure 6.19   Channel analysis of the BAA share price in July 1993 from daily data

level than the previous one, thereby confirming that the inner channel has changed direction by bouncing off the lower outer boundary. Thus the share is now at a buying point at 368p.

This has to be compared with the buying point of 365.5p which was deduced from the weekly data. Although we are having to pay a slightly higher price, we have much more confidence in the future price direction because of the fact that we have seen three troughs in the daily price which define quite clearly the fact that the lower boundary in the inner channel has changed direction.

January 1994 (Figure 6.20)

At this point in time, just as was the case with weekly data, we can see that the inner channel is clearly rising, and the outer channel, which was horizontal in the previous example, is now rising again. The inner channel is at, or very close to, the most likely position of the upper boundary of the outer channel and therefore expected to bounce down again.

The price reaches the top of the inner channel on 29th December 1993 at 532p. After falling back slightly, the price arrived again at 532p in early January, fell back again and then reached 535.5p before falling slightly again. This failure of the minor peaks to rise much beyond 530p is a sign

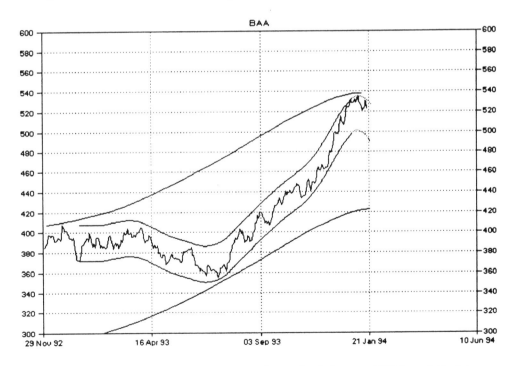

Figure 6.20 Channel analysis of the BAA share price in January 1994 from daily data

that the short term trends have run out of steam, and that we are probably at the high point for the time being. The confirmation of this will come if the next peak is at a lower level than 535.5p. This next peak is formed by the price rising to 530p on 18th January from a low of 520.5p and then falling back to 528p on 19th January. We can now be confident that the price will not go higher, and can sell at this point.

Taking the previous buying decision into account, we have seen a rise from 368p to 528p for a gain of 43%. This is a few percent better than was obtained using weekly data for the channels, but has occurred over a period of time one month less than was the case with weekly data, giving a much better weekly return.

July/August 1994 (Figure 6.21)

With the formation of the trough in the share price of 441p on 24th June 1994, the price is at the lower boundary of the inner channel which is still falling at the same slope as a few weeks earlier. The next trough to be formed after this was at 441.5p on 28th June. That this trough was not lower than the previous one is an encouraging sign that the inner channel may be reaching its lowest point for the time being. As in previous cases, we are waiting for a further trough to be formed to see if it is at a higher level than the previous one, which can then be taken as a positive sign of channel reversal.

After a few days of rising from the low of 441.5p, the price falls back to 444.5p on 4th July 1994. This becomes a trough by virtue of the rise the next day to 447.5p.

Thus we have seen a succession of three troughs, close together, but each at a higher level, at a point in time when the price is close to the lower boundary of the outer channel. This has to be taken as a sign that the price has reversed, and we can now buy on 5th July 1994 at a price of 447.5p.

When weekly data were used for the analysis, the buying point was given at a price of 480p, and we considered that this was too far up from the lower boundary to be other than a risky investment, since the upper boundary of the outer channel was running at a level of about 540p. Thus with daily data, we have a much greater potential for profit if the price rises to 540p, since this would give us a gain of over 20%.

Finally, it is necessary to draw attention to the different profit potential for the circumstances when a buying point is reached where the outer channel is rising, running horizontally or falling, and assuming that the price rises from the bottom of the outer channel to the top of the outer channel over the course of time. If we assume that the outer channel depth is say 100p, then the simplest case is that where the outer channel is running horizontally. If the price rises from the bottom to the top, then obviously the rise in price will be 100p over whatever period of time it takes to cross the channel.

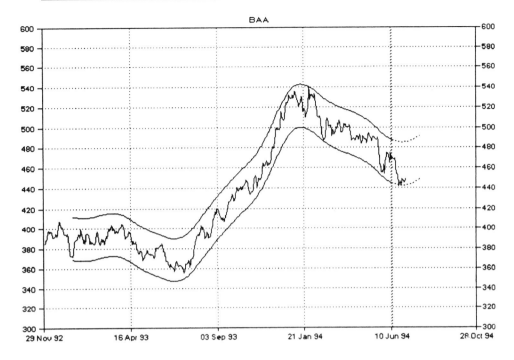

Figure 6.21 Channel analysis of the BAA share price in July 1994 from daily data

If the outer channel is rising, then as well as this rise of 100p, we have to add the amount by which the outer channel has risen from the point where the price rises from its lower boundary to the point where the price reaches the upper boundary. Obviously, the steeper the slope in the outer channel, the greater will be the rise in share price, while the longer the price takes to make its rise, the further will the outer channel have risen during this period. Such cases are the optimum for investment.

On the other hand, when the outer channel is falling, we have to deduct from the rise of 100p due to the channel depth the amount by which the outer channel has fallen by the time the price reaches the upper boundary. In bad cases where either the channel is falling steeply or the price is taking its time to move, the price at the upper boundary may well be less than it was earlier at the lower boundary. Thus the investor should never invest if the outer channel is seen to be falling. It is acceptable to invest when the channel is running horizontally, provided the investor watches the price constantly and exits at the first sign of danger.

7

The Relationship between Moving Averages and Channels

AVERAGES AS TEMPLATES FOR CHANNELS

Although in the last chapter we treated moving averages and channel analysis as quite different techniques which lead to broadly similar results for the prediction of share price movement, they are fundamentally the same. Moving averages are mathematical quantities which are calculated from original data and serve to remove fluctuations of increasing periodicity as the span of the average increases. The drawing of channels so as to enclose the share price data is the result of an averaging process carried out by the interplay between the eye and the brain. The channel which encloses the most minor fluctuations represents the movement caused by fluctuations of longer periodicity than those within the channel. Therefore this channel which is being drawn is removing the same fluctuations as an average of appropriate span, i.e. of similar span to the periodicity of the fluctuations which are being removed. The drawing of outer channels so as to enclose the peaks and troughs in the previously drawn channel can be continued until there are not enough peaks and troughs left in the outermost channels to be able to draw a final enclosing channel with any accuracy. We should see now that each successive outer channel is performing the function of a moving average of an appropriate span.

The relationship between channels and averages becomes more apparent if a centre line is drawn through a channel. This centre line now represents the combined effect of all the cycles of longer periodicity than those contained by the channel. Since we have now produced a line rather than a channel, we now have something which can be directly compared with a moving average line.

It should now be obvious that it is only a matter of selecting the correct span for an average so that it allows through all those periodicities which are represented by the centre line of the channel. By this process, and of

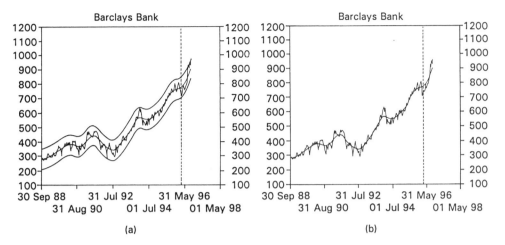

Figure 7.1 (a) Freehand channel with centre line added. (b) Calculated moving average showing similarity to channel centre line

course allowing for human inaccuracy in drawing channels, we should arrive at almost identical lines. This is illustrated in Figure 7.1(a) and (b).

We can now see that the computation and plotting of a moving average gives us a good starting point for drawing a channel. No longer are we faced with a sheet of paper which is blank except for the share price movements—we already have in place a template for the channel. Since the prime requirement for a channel is that the depth is kept constant and that most of the fluctuations of the data are contained within the upper and lower boundaries, it is now a simple task to draw these boundaries so that they fulfil these two requirements exactly. Each boundary has to be exactly the same vertical distance above or below the average line at each point.

Having done this, we are faced with a slight difference between the channel which we have produced from a moving average and the channel we have drawn freehand. In the latter case we would draw the channel as far in time as the last data point, and then proceed to project it into the future. An average terminates half a span back in time, and so we still have to apply some freehand drawing to bring it up to the time position of the last data point, and more freehand drawing to project it into the future. The stages in this process are shown in Figure 7.2.

This is an important fact—even by calculating channels directly from the data by using a calculator or computer, we cannot avoid a freehand extrapolation into the future. Even the most sophisticated computer program would be faced with this problem—extensive curve-fitting procedures which will extrapolate the channels into the future cannot be more than a "best guess" process, and certainly cannot predict the unpredictable, i.e. the random movement associated with share price data. To all intents and

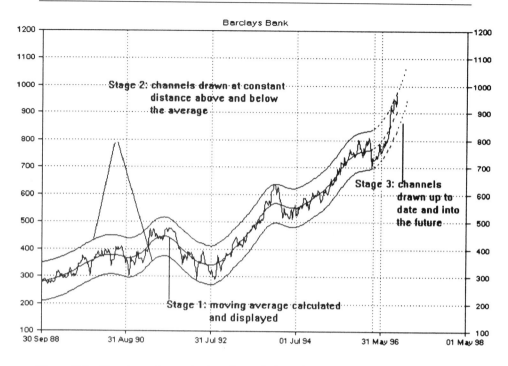

Figure 7.2 The stages in producing channels by calculation. The moving average is calculated and displayed and the channels drawn at a constant distance above and below the average. They are then extrapolated to the time of the latest data point and on into the future

purposes, a freehand extrapolation of a channel into the future is as good as any computer prediction. Where the computer scores is in the accuracy of the channels it can produce over the time period of the historical data but excluding any lag forced on the calculation by the span of the particular average involved.

COMPUTING CHANNEL DEPTHS

Now that the computer or calculator is giving us a great deal of help in deriving the shape of the various channels in which we are interested, it is natural to wish to see if we can also get help with calculating the depths of the channels. If that turns out to be the case, we will have a very rapid method of drawing channels accurately up to the time at which the average terminates. The answer is that we can calculate these depths, although rather more extensive calculations are required. For this reason it is not recommended that the investor attempts these calculations unless he has a computer or a programmable calculator. The calculation is based on a consideration of the scatter of the actual data points around the plotted moving average. A quantity called the "standard deviation" is a measurement of this scatter, and from this we can work out where to place the channels so as to contain whichever proportion of the data movement that we wish.

To be able to calculate the standard deviation of the points around the moving average line, we first of all have to tabulate the distance of each point from the moving average with which it is associated, i.e. with the average placed half a span back in time, as we have been doing throughout this book. Fortunately, those investors who have been taking note of the value of moving average differences for determining short term cycles in the data have already done this! The values which we use to calculate the standard deviation are simply the moving average differences, and we showed exactly how to derive these in Table 4.2 in Chapter 4.

The arithmetic is now tedious, since we have to calculate another column of values. These are simply the square of each moving average difference. To do this, we can present Table 4.2 again with this additional column added, as shown in Table 7.1.

Finally, it is not the individual values of moving average difference or the square of a moving average difference that we require, but the total of each of these. We therefore have to add together all the values in the column headed "Average difference", and add together all the values in the column headed "Square". Note that we must take into account the *sign* of the values in the moving average difference column, so that we add or subtract the next number to the running total as we move down the column. In the squares column all the numbers are positive. At the end of this exercise we have two totals, one of which, the sum of the squares, should be quite large. The final value that we need in order to calculate the standard deviation is the *number* of items which we have added together to produce these two totals, i.e. the number of moving average difference values which we used, in this case 19.

We can now calculate a quantity called the variance:

$$\text{variance} = (S(Y^2) - S^2(Y)/N)/(N-1)$$

where S stands for "sum of". The standard deviation is simply the square root of this number:

$$\text{standard deviation} = SQR(\text{variance})$$

The quantity $S^2(Y)$ is the square of the sum of the average differences. The quantity $S(Y^2)$ is the sum of the squares of the individual average differences. N is the number of moving average differences which were added together.

Taking the values in Table 7.1, we get the sum of the average differences of the 19 values, i.e. $S(Y) = 14.6$, therefore $S^2(Y)/N = 14.6^2/19 = 213.16/19 = 11.219$. The sum of the squares, i.e. $S(Y^2)$, is 2486.36. From this the

Table 7.1 Calculation of five-week standard deviation. The data are presented as in Table 4.2, and the square of each average difference placed in the final column

Value	Subtract	Five-week total	Five-week average	Aligned average	Average difference	Square
49	x					
17	x					
18	x			33.4		
23	x			35.8		
60	x	167	33.4	42.4	17.6	309.76
61	x	179	35.8	48.6	12.4	153.76
50	x	212	42.4	56.2	−6.2	38.44
49	x	243	48.6	57.0	−8.0	64.0
61	x	281	56.2	59.0	2.0	4.0
64	x	285	57.0	65.4	−1.4	1.96
71	x	295	59.0	65.6	5.4	29.16
82	x	327	65.4	67.2	14.8	219.04
50	x	328	65.6	69.6	−19.6	384.16
69	x	336	67.2	64.0	5.0	25.0
76	x	348	69.6	54.0	22.0	484.0
43	x	320	64.0	53.6	−10.6	112.36
32	x	270	54.0	47.8	−15.8	249.64
48	x	268	53.6	38.6	9.4	88.36
40	x	239	47.8	36.0	4.0	16.0
30	x	193	38.6	32.8	−2.8	7.84
30		180	36.0	30.8	−0.8	0.64
16		164	32.8	32.8	−16.8	282.24
38		154	30.8	34.0	4.0	16.0
50		164	32.8			
36		170	34.0			
Totals					14.6	2486.36

variance is 137.5 and so the square root of this is the standard deviation, 11.7. The channel depth which we can calculate from this value of standard deviation depends upon what percentage of the data points we wish to enclose within the channel. It is a mathematical fact that about 68% of the points will lie within the channel which is drawn one standard deviation above and below the moving average, 95.5% will lie within a channel two standard deviations above and below the average, and 99.7% will lie within a channel three standard deviations above and below the average. The last value is overkill, because only three points in 1000 will lie outside the channel, and we have frequently said that it is permissible to have a small number of points penetrating the channel. For this reason, two standard deviations above and below the average will be perfectly satisfactory. For the data in Table 7.1, therefore, the channel depth which will

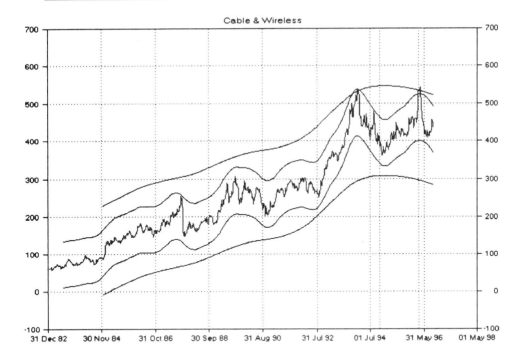

Figure 7.3 Channels produced automatically by the MICROVEST 5.0 program

accommodate 95.5% of the movement is 46.8, i.e. 23.4 (two standard deviations) above and below the average itself.

What we have outlined here is a method of calculating and plotting the channels accurately, and the result of doing this is shown by the plot in Figure 7.3 produced by the MICROVEST 5.0 program.

MULTIPLE AVERAGES

When a number of cycles of different wavelength are present at the same time in a share price movement, then the troughs and peaks occur at different times. There will be occasions when the troughs or peaks of a number of different cycles happen to coincide, and these occasions are major decision points. The subsequent movement of the share price will be exaggerated, since for a short period of time all of these cycles will be acting in concert, i.e. the amplitudes of the cycles will be additive.

When a number of moving averages of increasing span is calculated and displayed, the presence of a number of cycles whose peaks and troughs are occurring at mostly different times will appear to give a jumble of such moving average lines. A closer inspection will show that they are not quite as jumbled up as first appears.

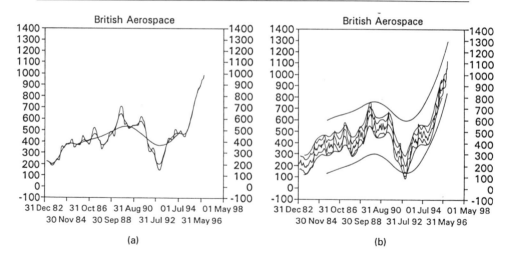

Figure 7.4 (a) Multiple averages do not convey information readily. (b) Channel analysis shows the same information in a way in which relationships are instantly visible

   With a computer that plots averages as different coloured lines, it might be slightly easier to see than with a monochrome display or a chart on paper, but each moving average oscillates about the next higher span average. Because of this oscillation, it is possible with practice to extract the relationships between the moving averages and hence the relationships between the cycles which they represent, but this is not easy. This is one area in which channel analysis scores heavily, because almost the same information about cycles is being presented, but in a form in which the relationships jump out at you. This is illustrated by the comparison between parts (a) and (b) of Figure 7.4.
   It is the depth allocated to channels which is the single most important fact that brings meaning to the data. Note that we can take a presentation such as that in Figure 7.4(b) and achieve the same somewhat confusing oscillation of the cycles by drawing a centre line down each channel. This is shown in Figure 7.5.
   This reverse approach then highlights an aspect of oscillating moving averages that might not otherwise be apparent. The constant depth requirement means that an inner channel when oscillating within the next outer channel should at its extreme movements reach points which are an equal distance above and below the centre line of the channel. Converting this behaviour into the behaviour of averages means that the extremities of the oscillation of an average about a longer span average should be more or less equal. Thus the oscillations of the averages have a symmetry that might not be obvious at first glance at Figure 7.4(a).

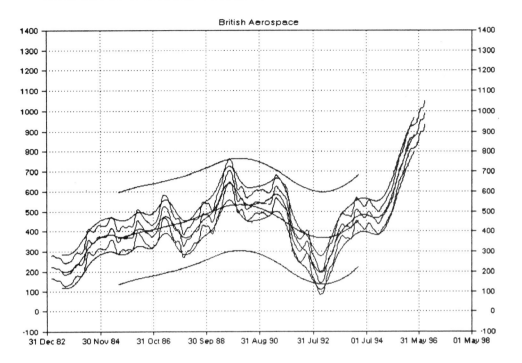

Figure 7.5 The centre lines drawn through each channel are virtually identical with the moving averages shown in Figure 7.4(a), and are equally difficult to analyse

The cycles present in share price data are normally well spaced in terms of wavelength. It would be most unusual to have cycles of say 20 weeks and 25 weeks present at the same time. If such a pair of cycles do appear to be present, they probably represent the same cycle which has changed its wavelength slightly in accordance with the variation discussed in the last chapter.

Because of this spacing of wavelengths, the number of averages we need to apply is quite limited. What we will find is that the appearance of a number of plotted moving averages is very similar.

This happens because, of course, a moving average allows through wavelengths greater than the span of that particular average. If a particular cycle is much longer in wavelength than the average which we have chosen, and there is no other cycle whose wavelength lies between these two values, then we can apply all of the possible averages between this initial value and the wavelength of the cycle with essentially the same result. As an example, suppose we have two cycles of 21-week and 51-week periodicity and no other cycle lying between these two values. We can apply a 21-week average to remove the 21-week cycle and display just the 51-week cycle plus any others of wavelength greater than 51 weeks. All

averages from 21-week up to 49-week will have this same effect of removing the 21-week cycle and leaving the 51-week cycle. The general
appearance of the result is the same with one important exception—the
points which are missing at the end of the average. This gap between the
last point of the average and the last data point increases as we increase
the span of the average. From the point of view of projecting channels
forward in time, we have more and more prediction to carry out as we
increase the span of the average from which the channels are derived. This
is illustrated in Figure 7.6, where four averages of increasing span applied
to British Aerospace data give almost the same line except for these extra
points at the end.

  The message is clear—when using moving averages to compute the
channels, use the shortest span which will produce a meaningful channel,
with the proviso that the random movement is eliminated, and that the
next channel to be produced in this way is significantly different from the
previous one. This latter requirement can be satisfied by making a large
jump in the span of the next average which will be applied once the first
good channel has been produced. In practice, taking GEC as an example,

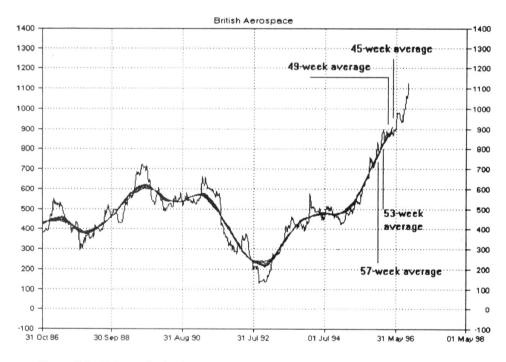

Figure 7.6 If the cycles in share price data are widely separated, many moving averages will appear identical except for the increasing loss of points at either end as the
span of the average increases

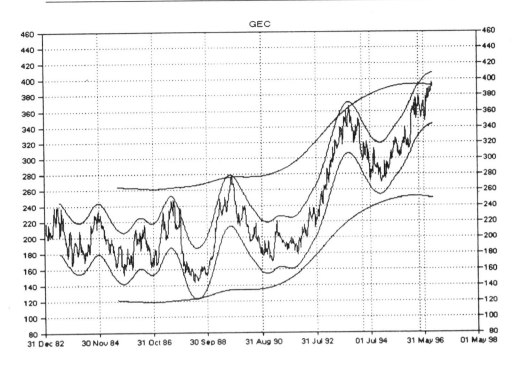

Figure 7.7   The channels produced for the GEC share price by using averages of one year (53 weeks) and five years (261 weeks) with the MICROVEST 5.0 program

the spacing of averages which would produce good channels would be 53 and 265 weeks, and the results of using these values are shown in Figure 7.7. An average with a shorter span than 53 weeks is not used in this case because of the absence of significant cycles of wavelength much less than one year.

Other values will be necessary for other shares, but this example gives an idea of the fairly wide spacing that will have to be used. Where there are cycles of significant amplitude with shorter wavelengths, then an average of shorter span such as 27 weeks may be used. This is shown in Figure 7.8 for BAT, with 27-week and 209-week averages being used.

Figures 7.7 and 7.8 illustrate the considerable help in channel analysis which is available when we have the computational facilities to calculate moving averages, moving average differences and standard deviations. This does not detract in any way from the value of channels which are drawn freehand by investors who do not have access to a computer. With experience and practice, there will be virtually no difference between the results obtained by such investors and their computerised colleagues. Where the latter score will be in convenience and the ability to do their own research in terms of experimenting with a wide variety of channels

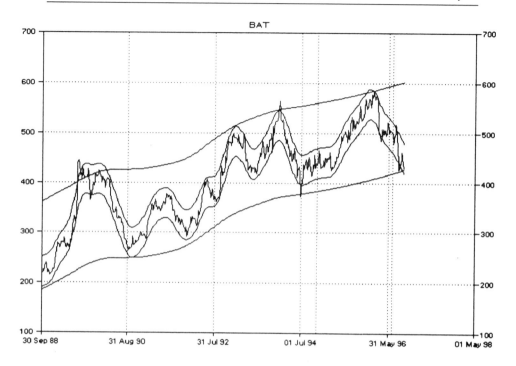

Figure 7.8 The channels produced for the BAT share price by using averages of 27 weeks and 209 weeks with the MICROVEST 5.0 program

and averages with the minimum of effort. They will still, at the end of the day, have to project their computer-produced channels into the future in order to predict investment decision points.

8

Turning Points in Share Prices

The most important lesson that can be learned in stock market investment is never to buck the trend. If the trend in a share price is headed downwards, then it is not safe to invest in that share until the trend has changed direction. It is vital that the investor does not anticipate the end of a trend, since the principle of variation in the periodicity and amplitude of the

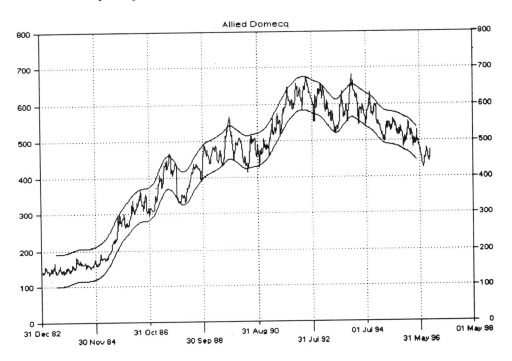

Figure 8.1 The Allied Domecq share price with a channel computed from the 53-week weighted average. The overlap, i.e. proportion of points allowed outside the boundaries, is 3.5%. Since the channel is based on a 53-week average, it terminates half a span, i.e. 27 weeks, before the latest data point

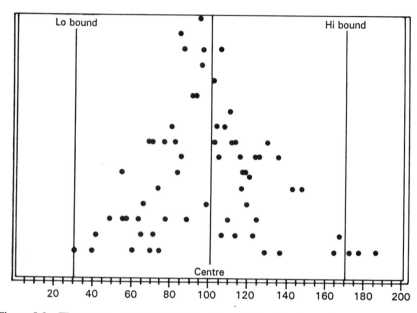

Figure 8.2 The scatter of the individual points within the above channel

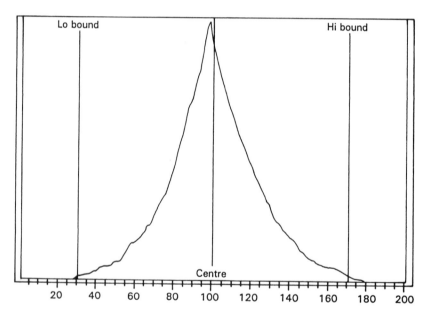

Figure 8.3 The data from Figure 8.2 converted into probabilities. The vertical axis is the probability that a point lies between a specified point on the horizontal axis and the channel boundary. No values are given to probability since it is the shape of the curve that is of interest. Note that there are low probabilities for points lying near the boundaries

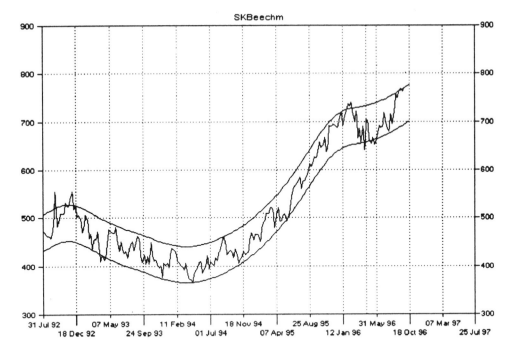

Figure 8.4 The gently curving channel in SmithKleinBeecham. Historically it can be seen to have turned on 15th April 1994 when the price bottomed out at 364p.

cycles that are present in the share price can mean that in extreme circumstances the predicted change may not occur. Even if circumstances are not extreme, the turning point may be delayed for a considerable number of weeks, during which the share price will continue to move in the adverse direction.

The prime safety factor that will prevent investors making such a mistake is discipline. Under no circumstances should an investment be made or sold until there is firm evidence that the trend which is being followed for the purposes of the investment has changed direction. The risk involved in trying to get in at the exact bottom of the market or get out at the exact top of the market is too high to be acceptable in return for the extra few pennies that will be squeezed out of the subsequent share price movement. The method of channel analysis is the most powerful available for predicting share prices and detecting turning points in share prices, and if the share has been chosen properly, the rise will be such that the loss of a few pence at either end is irrelevant. Always remember that the predictive ability of channel analysis has to be used in one way only, and that is to predict turning points so that they will be recognised as, or just after, they occur. Channel analysis prediction must never be used to take up an investment position in advance of the predicted event. The preservation of

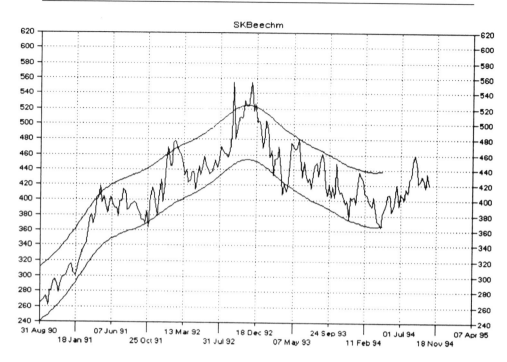

Figure 8.5 Because of the lag in a centred average, the true position of the channel at 15th April 1994 cannot be determined until 27 weeks later on 21st October 1994

capital has to take precedence over any gambling instinct that the investor is fighting to control.

Two types of turning points occur in share prices, irrespective of whether long term or shorter term cycles are being followed. The turning point can be gently curved, with numbers of troughs or peaks behaving impeccably and falling almost exactly on the gently curving channel boundary. Because the channel is curving gradually, the investor will be able to get in or get out within a few pennies of the bottom or top of that particular trend. The rate of change of the share price is low, and therefore the investor has the luxury of a number of weeks after the bottom or top has been passed before he starts to lose more than a few pennies out of the new rising or falling trend. The turning point can also be extremely sharp, with peaks or troughs penetrating the boundaries of the channel to a much greater extent than would be predicted from the previous shape of the channels. The rate of change of the share price is enormous, and rises or falls of 5% or even 10% can occur over the course of a week. The last thing the investor has is the luxury of time. A delay of more than a week in taking a decision to buy or sell can be extremely costly. The most costly of course is to delay the selling point, since money already acquired, at least on paper, is being lost. Delaying the buying point is not quite as disastrous,

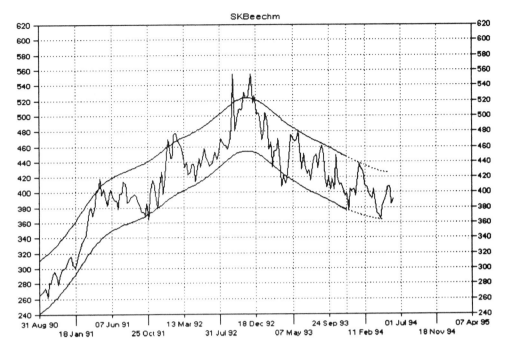

Figure 8.6 The position of the channel as estimated on 3rd June 1994. There are signs that the rate of fall of the channel is slowing down. If we assume that the significant trough on 15th April must lie on the lower channel boundary, then the channel curvature has to be decreased as shown

since a gain will still be made out of the rise which is now under way. Because of this problem with selling, an additional technique must be applied to that of channel analysis, and that is the use of stop losses. The ways in which these can be applied are discussed in Chapter 10.

SCATTER OF POINTS WITHIN A CHANNEL

So far we have looked at channel boundaries in the simplest way. They are drawn so as to limit the number of points that lie outside or on the boundary. When drawn by computer, a starting point for the number of points which lie outside the boundaries is about 3.5% of the total number that are present in the data. Thus with a plot of 1000 points, the computer would allow 35 points to lie outside the boundaries. When drawn manually rather than by computer, the investor allows a small number to lie outside the boundaries, and is instinctively reaching a value of between 1% and 5%. The value is not critical. If it is increased, then the channel gets narrower, with more peaks projecting outside the boundaries. If it is

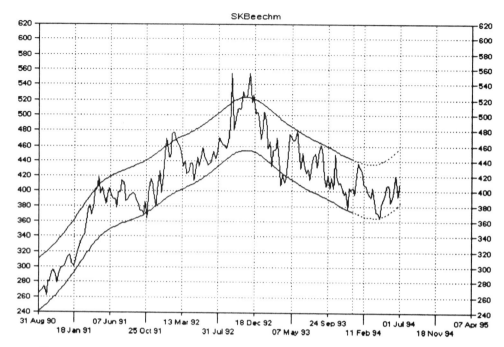

Figure 8.7 The position of the channel as estimated on 1st July 1994. The addition of four more data points has given a decreasing curve to the channel at its last calculated point. An extrapolation of this curve gives a turning point in the channel. There are also some recent minor peaks which support the fact that the channel has changed direction

decreased, eventually we reach a point where a small number of points, perhaps even just one point, lie exactly on the boundary, and none outside it. The channel will get wider as this number decreases.

The reason why 3.5% is a useful starting number is the requirement to have a balance between only one point at a boundary and many points outside the boundary. In the first case, the probability of a future point lying at or beyond the boundary is low, so that we would never predict a bounce in price from the boundary, since prices would lie more towards the centre of the channel. In the second case we would have a multitude of occasions where the price reached the boundary, and only a proportion of these would be genuine turning points in which the price would then retreat. The others would proceed some way beyond the boundary before turning.

A better appreciation of this point can be obtained by looking at the scatter of points within a channel, i.e. how far they lie from the upper and lower boundaries.

Figure 8.1 shows the data for weekly closing prices of Allied Domecq since the beginning of 1982. A channel based on the 53-week weighted average has been drawn, with the overlap of channel boundaries being set

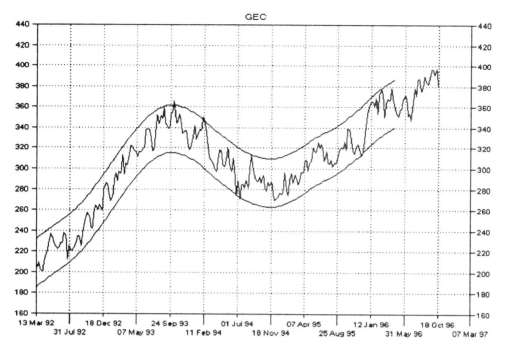

Figure 8.8 The gently curving channel in the GEC share price, using a 53-week weighted average

at 3.5%. Note that the channels terminate 27 weeks before the last data point. This is because the channel is based on a moving average, and the last true calculated point of the centred average is at this point half a span back in time, as discussed in Chapter 4. When we come to look more closely at channel turning points, we will see that these depend upon a prediction of how the channel has progressed over this last half-span.

The plot in Figure 8.2 is derived from this, and shows the location of each point of the data relative to the channel boundaries as a percentage distance, with the channel width being 200 units. Thus the centre corresponds to the point 100. There are only a few points lying outside the channel boundaries. The vertical scale represents numbers of points at the particular distance from the centre of the channel.

Most points lie towards the centre of the channel, and the numbers of points decrease as we get closer to the boundaries.

A more meaningful discussion can follow the conversion of the data in Figure 8.2 into probabilities. This is done in Figure 8.3. It is the shape rather than exact values for probability that is important. The curve represents the probability that a point lies between a specified place on the horizontal axis and the nearest channel boundary. The probability is highest at the centre of the channel, and as we approach the boundaries this

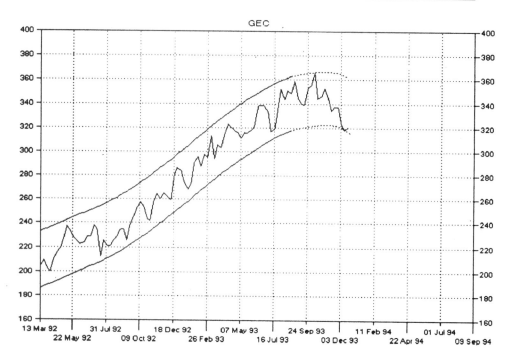

Figure 8.9 The calculated channels in GEC on 17th December 1993. This is the first point at which the fall in price would violate the lower boundary. The extrapolated section of the channel must be bent in order to accommodate both the peak on 8th October and the latest price of 320p

probability decreases rapidly. This is the crucial point about channel analysis. **Channel boundaries represent low probability areas**, since the price spends very little time in these regions. This is easily confirmed by inspection—the price does not run along channel boundaries but rebounds quite rapidly. **Channel centres represent high probabilities**, and the price spends more time in this part of the channel.

If a price is currently at the boundary, and therefore in a low probability area, then the probability remains low that it will still be there the next week or next day. The most likely outcome is that the price therefore retreats to a place where the probability is higher, i.e. back towards the centre of the channel.

We now come back to the major difficulty with channels, especially computed ones, and one which requires the most careful analysis. This is the question of filling in the gap between the last computed position of the channel and the present time or near future. As we shall see when looking more closely at this question, the channel may well have already changed direction, so that we would be in error in assuming the channel is running in the same direction as it was at the last computed point.

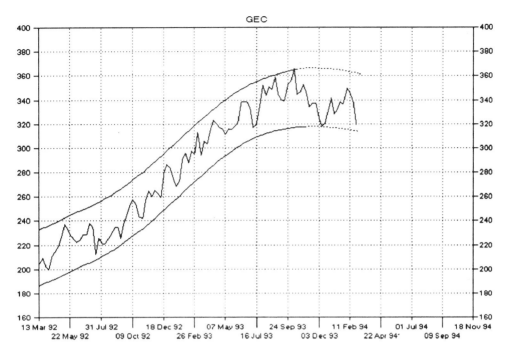

Figure 8.10   By 25th February 1994 we are now convinced that the channel has turned
down because the trough must sit on the lower boundary

GENTLY CURVED CHANNELS

The SmithKleinBeecham share price is one which shows a very rounded
turn in the 53-week channel, as shown in Figure 8.4. Looking back from
the futures, it can be seen that the channel bottomed out with the trough in
the price at 364p, on 15th April 1994. This was at week 589 from the start
of the data.

Since the channel is based on a 53-week average, it would be 27 weeks
hence from the 15th April, i.e. 21st October 1994, before the calculation of
the channel gave its true position on 15th April. This position is shown in
Figure 8.5.

Thus between the points of 15th April and 21st October we are put in
the position of having to deduce the position and direction of the channel
boundaries before an investment can be made.

Figure 8.6 shows the estimated latest position of the 53-week channel on
3rd June 1994. Prior to that point the channel had been falling quite
steadily. The feature that is vital to our estimation that the rate of fall of
the channel might be slowing is the significant trough formed on 15th
April. This cannot be considered to be a minor trough since it has been

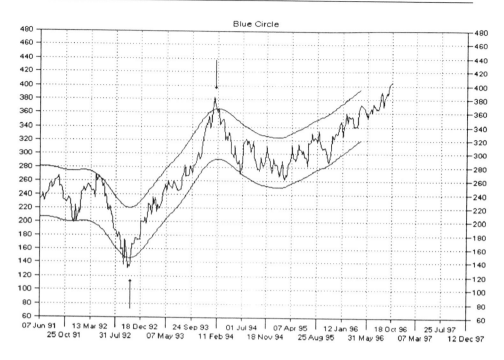

Figure 8.11 The Blue Circle share price shows two sharp turning points in the 53-weeek channel on 2nd October 1992 and 21st January 1994

formed by a fall from the top of the channel with hardly any hesitation. Since we consider it to be so significant, we must also assume that it lies on the lower channel boundary. If this is the case, then the rate of fall of the channel must be decreased, i.e. the channel must be bent from its previous direction in order to achieve this.

This is about as far as we can go with the prediction at this point, which is of course some seven weeks past the point at which, well into the future (Figure 8.4), we were able to estimate that the channel had turned. This is still an excellent prediction since we are only about a quarter of the way across the gap of 27 weeks until the turning point is known with absolute certainty.

Naturally, as we proceed towards the point (21st October 1994) at which we will know the turning point with total certainty, our estimation of the channel position should improve with each new week's data point that can be entered into the channel calculation.

In Figure 8.7 is seen the position as estimated a further four weeks on, on 1st July 1994. The extra four data points when entered into the channel calculation show that the downward trend of the channel is decreasing rapidly. An extrapolation of this slope shows it to have bottomed out, i.e. the channel has changed direction. We still need additional confirmation

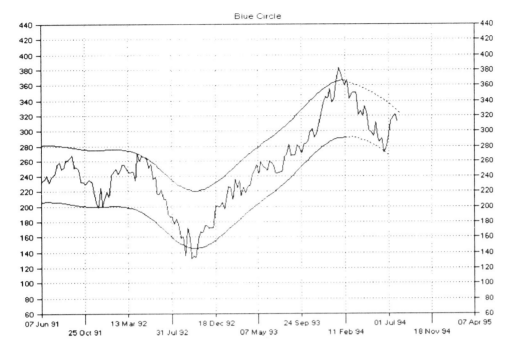

Figure 8.12 It is not until 29th July 1995 that calculation of the channels gives us the true picture on 21st January 1994, showing that the channel had topped out

of this fact, and this is given by the two troughs which occur after the significant one on 15th April. These lie close to the extrapolated, upward trending boundary, giving us extra confidence that the channel has now changed direction.

This is a case where attention was focused on features lying on just one boundary, the lower one in this case, in order to confirm that the channel had changed direction. It was not necessary to pay attention to the channel depth. There are, however, cases where features at the opposite side of the channel can be used to confirm its turn because of the necessity of maintaining a constant depth.

This approach is shown by the example of GEC. Figure 8.8 shows that there was a gently curved channel which turned on 8th October 1993 with a peak price of 365.5p.

It was not until 10 weeks after this peak price, i.e. on 17th December 1993, that the first indications were given that the channel may have topped out (Figure 8.9). This follows from the fact that the price has fallen to 320p. If the previous constant depth of the channel is to be maintained and the upper boundary is to go through the peak of 365.5p, then the price level of 320p would be well below the lower boundary. Since we are striving to limit the number of points which lie outside the channel

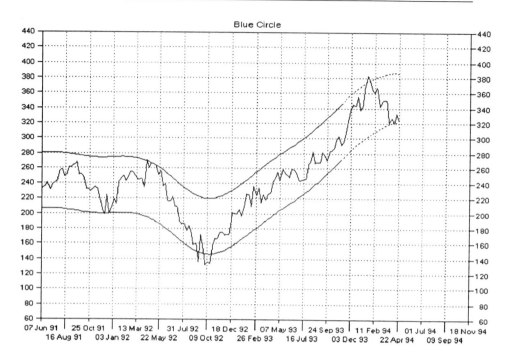

Figure 8.13 This is the first time that there is a faint indication that the 53-week channel in Blue Circle might have begun to change direction. This is because we cannot accommodate both the peak and the latest share price within the same channel boundary without bending it

boundary, the only way to keep both the peak at or near the upper boundary, and the price of 320p at or near the lower boundary, is by forcing the channel into a bend with its extreme at the peak of 365.5p. Thus we have come to the conclusion that the channel has changed direction, but only by taking into account both boundaries of the channel and the requirement for a constant depth, unlike the previous case where looking at just one boundary gave us all the information we required. Note that since a trough has not yet been formed in the share price, we would have to keep increasing the bend in the channel each week as long as the share price kept falling in order to keep the latest price at the boundary. Thus the channel boundary is not fixed until we get a trough formed which will be assumed to lie on the boundary.

This position is reached a few weeks later, as shown in Figure 8.10. We now have almost total confidence that the channel has changed direction because the lower boundary is fixed by the trough which has been formed.

It was not until 27 weeks have passed from the position of the peak price, i.e. on 15th April 1994, that the calculation would give us the true position on 8th October 1993, showing that the channel had topped out.

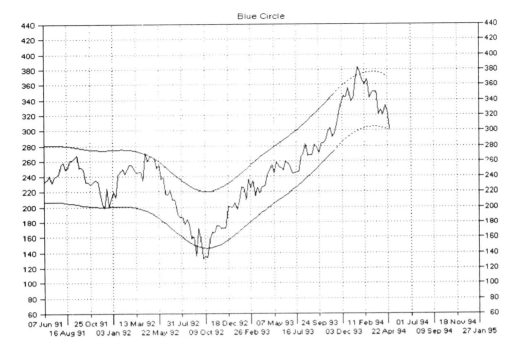

Figure 8.14 A week later we have much more confidence that the channel has changed direction

These two examples have illustrated the careful analysis which must be carried out to decide when a channel has changed direction from a falling one to a rising one, or from a rising one to a falling one. Note carefully the general method of extending the channel gradually. We look for the next peak or trough which will enable us to extend the upper or lower boundary, as the case may be, and then seek to extend the opposite boundary while keeping a constant depth by looking for the next trough or peak. If these fall on the projected boundary, all well and good, otherwise we have to take a decision as to whether the boundary should be curved more or less in order to accommodate this new trough or peak. If a major accommodation is required, then we need the next peak or trough to confirm that the channel is changing direction.

SHARP TURNING POINTS

Places where the channel changes direction over the course of just a few weeks see such rapid rises and falls in share prices that they test the principles of channel analysis to the limit. The simple application of the change in direction of a moving average is useless to deal with such sharp

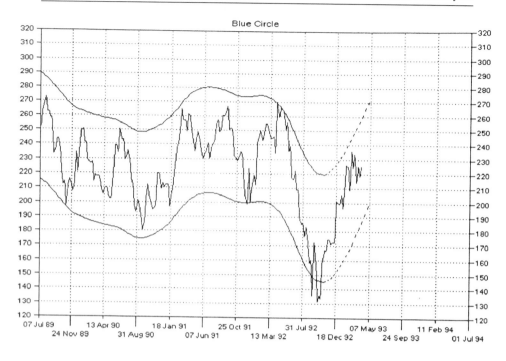

Figure 8.15   It was not until 9th April 1993 that the true turning point in the channel on 2nd October 1992 could be calculated with 100% certainty

peaks and troughs since by the time the average changes direction, the price could, in a bad case, have risen or fallen by as much as 20%. Sharp turning points must be seen as being extremely dangerous for the investor, wiping out a large proportion of his capital unless the most stringent precautions are taken. The luxury of waiting for a number of peaks and troughs several weeks apart and spread out over a reasonable time so that the channel can be well defined is not available. There might only be two peaks and one trough to define a channel which is rapidly bottoming out, or two troughs and a peak to define a channel which is topping out, and therefore rapid decisions will have to be taken.

Fortunately, there is a way around this, since these events give us a very short warning which we must recognise. If we are keeping weekly data, *a sharp rise which is much sharper than has been the norm for that particular share will usually occur.* This rise will not only be rapid, *but will take us well through the projected channel boundary.* This will happen because we have projected channels on the basis of the previous smooth progressions of the share prices, so any violent movement must of necessity penetrate these channels. It is this unexpected penetration of the channel or channels that tells us that weekly data will no longer be sufficient to track the share price closely enough. This means that we must always have available

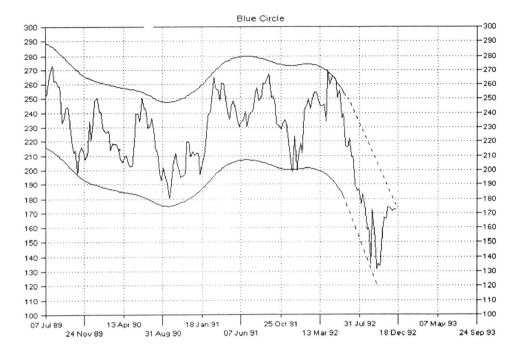

Figure 8.16 Even on 11th December 1992, 10 weeks after the actual turn in the channel, we would still come to the conclusion that it is falling

the daily newspaper which carries that share price, because it will be necessary to do some work in gathering daily prices for the past few weeks to be able to focus in on our sudden rapid rise in order to draw channels or trend lines of shorter cyclicality than we have been following so far.

The chart of Blue Circle shown in Figure 8.11 is an example where there are two sharp turning points, in October 1992 and January 1994. In both cases the difficulty is that there are no peaks or troughs running near the boundaries, i.e. the price is running down the middle part of the channel. Thus there are no features to enable us to extrapolate the boundary accurately.

Taking the turning point on 21st January 1994, it is not until 27 weeks have passed that the turn in the channel can be established from the calculation. This position is shown in Figure 8.12. The first point prior to that accurate calculation when there was any indication that the channel might have changed direction was on 22nd April 1994, as shown in Figure 8.13. By the following week, 29th April, as shown in Figure 8.14, we are much more confident that the channel has changed direction. Unfortunately this is some 15 weeks after the true turning point, much too long a delay to be of any use.

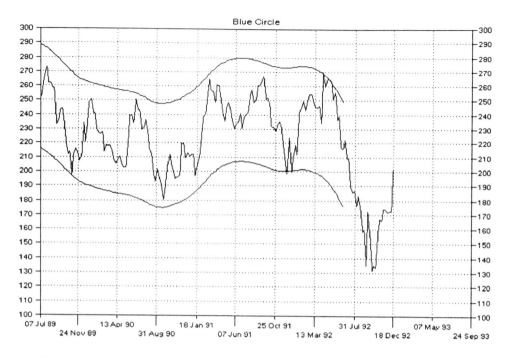

Figure 8.17   On 18th December 1992, 11 weeks after the actual turn in the channel, we would see a slight indication of a change in the rate of fall of the channel

We have the same situation with the rapid change in direction in October 1992. Figure 8.15 shows that it was not until 9th April 1993 that the calculation would give us the true picture on 2nd October 1992, showing that the channel had changed direction.

Taking a view on 11th December 1992, as shown in Figure 8.16, we would still conclude that the channel was headed downwards, since there is no indication of any bend in the calculated channel, and no feature of peak or trough that would give an indication that the direction has to be changed. However, a week later on 18th December (Figure 8.17), there is a sign that the channel slope is decreasing, although there are still no features that would give any added confidence to this interpretation. Thus, even 10 weeks after the actual turn in the channel, we are still faced with only a slight possibility that the downtrend has changed direction, but this is so slight as to make any investment at this point a wild gamble which we should not take.

The delay we have seen with sharp turning points when weekly data are used can be overcome to a considerable extent by using daily data. Taking the January 1994 turning point in Blue Circle, the daily data are shown in Figure 8.18 as on 24th February 1994, i.e. a month after we know the actual turn occurred from the historical viewpoint. The price fall to a point well

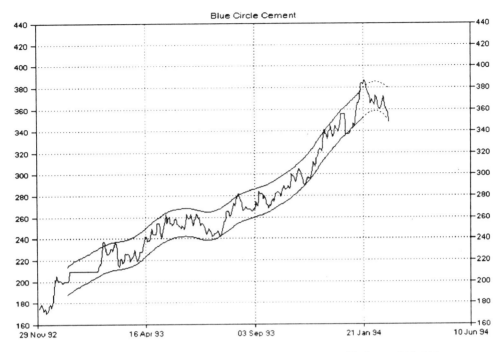

Figure 8.18 Channels produced from daily data for Blue Circle on 24th February 1994. The fall in price to a point well below the previous direction of the channel indicates that the channel has changed direction

below the inner channel boundary must mean that the latter has changed its slope considerably. We therefore feel that the latter is approaching its turning point.

Just over a week later, on 7th March (Figure 8.19), a significant trough had been formed in the share price which we must assume lies on the lower boundary of the inner channel. In order to accommodate this, and to allow the previous peak to lie close to or just outside the boundary, we have to reverse the channel direction at the position of the peak in January. The knock-on effect of this is that the longer term 53-week channel, transcribed as shown to this figure, must also change direction at the peaks in January.

By using daily data, therefore, we have come to the conclusion that both the short term and long term trends in the Blue Circle share price have topped out. This conclusion was reached only eight weeks after the event, as opposed to the long delay to 29th April that we had to suffer with weekly data.

The same advantage can be shown for the turning point in October 1992. The position with daily data on 28th October 1992 is shown in Figure 8.20. The price has risen to a level that takes it above the previous

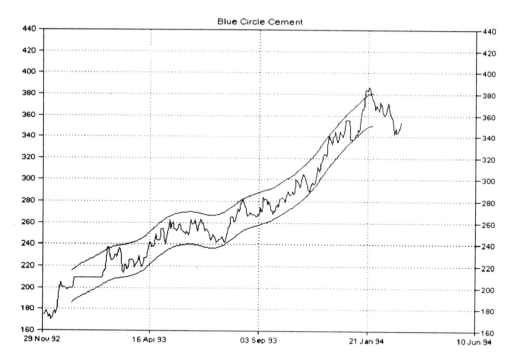

Figure 8.19 The position on 7th March 1994. The trough which has been formed now gives us a location for the lower boundary. This confirms that it changed direction at the peak in January 1994

downward path of the channel. This necessitates a revision of the channel, giving it a lesser slope. Thus we have the first indication that the channel may be about to change direction.

Just over a week later, on 9th November (Figure 8.21), the turn in the calculated channel can be seen quite clearly. By taking into account the peak that has been formed we are able to deduce with high confidence that the channel must have changed direction, probably at the point where the lowest trough occurred in October 1992. This change in direction of the channel will eventually lead us to the conclusion that the outer, 53-week channel has also changed direction. Thus we are being given the nod for an investment in a recently formed rising trend only five weeks after the trend can be shown to have changed direction from the historical perspective. When only weekly data were used, it was early 1993 before it became apparent that the channel was now rising.

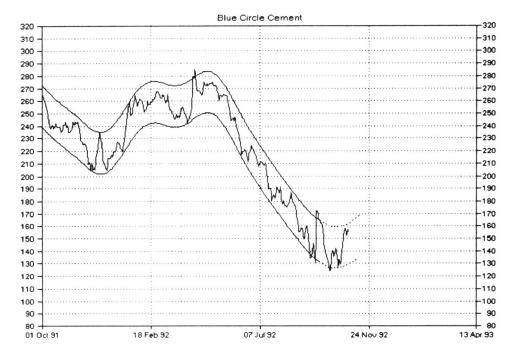

Figure 8.20   Channels produced from daily data for Blue Circle on 28th October 1992. The rise in price to a point well above the previous direction of the channel indicates that the channel has changed, or is about to change, direction

TURNING POINT SYMMETRY

For a small time window centred at the channel turning point we find that there is a high degree of symmetry. By this we mean that where the channel was falling and changes direction, the new upward path is virtually a mirror image of the previous downward path. The same applies to channels which rise and then fall. The amount of symmetry is at its highest for the shorter trends, but can get distorted for longer term trends. A closer look at the turning points in BAT as shown in Figure 8.22 brings home this point. The channel is based on a 53-week average.

This fact is very useful when we have come to the conclusion that a channel has changed direction but before we have enough data to calculate its true position. As a first stab at the new direction of the channel, we can simply draw in with dotted lines a channel rising at the same rate as the rate of fall of the previous section, as long as we draw it in such a position that the transition from falling to rising is a smooth one, with a curvature not too dissimilar from that which we have seen in practice for the same share on earlier occasions, or even in the charts of the other shares.

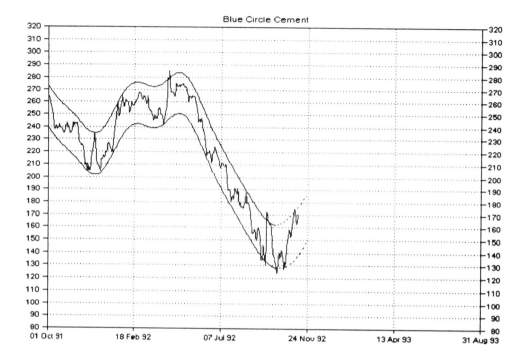

Figure 8.21 The position on 9th November 1992. The peak which has been formed now gives us a location for the upper boundary. This confirms that it changed direction at the trough in October 1992

Once this stage has been completed we can then make an adjustment up or down where the data cannot be accommodated by this first effort. In the absence of any other data, this represents our best effort at predicting the near-future direction of the channel.

We can now bring together the various strands of the estimation of channel turning points into one logical sequence of events which we should follow each time:

1. Assuming we are using the calculation method where channels are based on a template derived from a moving average, we plot these channels as far as the last true point, which will be half a span back in time.
2. We extrapolate the channels to the present time, i.e. the same point in time as the last data point, by drawing smooth curves, maintaining the same rate of change of curvature as was obvious in the last few true points of the channel.
3. If no data points violate the channel boundaries in this extrapolated section, then we have gone as far as we can. If the extrapolation shows the latest position of the channel to be running horizontally, i.e. it is at a

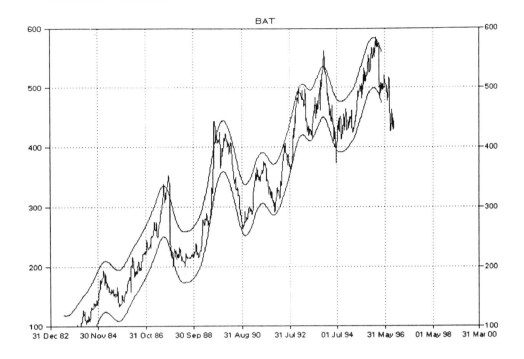

Figure 8.22 Channels produced by a 53-week moving average in the BAT share price showing a high degree of symmetry at the turning points

turning point, we draw a mirror image from this point onwards as a best guess at the new direction of the channel for the immediate future.

4. If data points violate either boundary of the extrapolated channel, we adjust the extrapolated channel up or down, retaining constant depth, so as to remove the violation as far as is possible.

5. If after following step 4 we have formed a turning point in the channel, then we can use the principle of symmetry to plot the new direction from the turning point onwards. If there are further violations of this symmetrical section, then it can be bent around the turning point so as to remove the violations.

It should also be noted that channel bottoms usually (but not always) occur at or very close to the position of a trough in the share price, while channel tops usually (but not always) occur at or very close to the position of a peak in the share price. Thus a predicted turning point can be moved slightly to bring about this coincidence on the grounds that it is the most probable position for the turning point.

We now have our best prediction for the position of the channel, enabling us to take a view of the future share price movement.

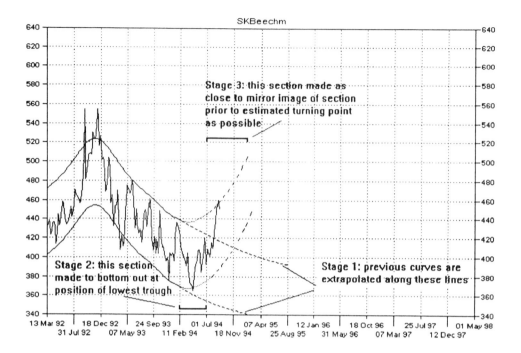

Figure 8.23   The logical sequence used to predict channels at turning points

If we are not using the calculated method, but have drawn the channel boundaries in manually according to the methods discussed earlier in Chapters 4 and 5, then we join this scheme at stage 2.

The procedure is shown graphically in Figure 8.23 for SmithKlein-Beecham at a point where the share price was 448p on 2nd September 1994. The rate of fall of the latest true section of the channel has started to diminish. Thus, an extrapolation by eye will cause the channel to bottom out at some time in the future. Taking into account the latest price, the channel must be bent upwards to accommodate it. The bend is made about the trough price, and the channel made to be a mirror image of the section prior to this trough. This gives us an estimate of the channel direction over the next few months.

How good a prediction this turned out to be can be seen by taking a view a year later in 1995, enabling us to calculate the real channel around the turning point in 1994. This is shown in Figure 8.24, where it can be seen that the predicted channel was a very good estimate of what actually happened.

Note that a computer program such as MICROVEST 5.0 will draw the extrapolated section of the channel between the last true calculated point of the channel and the present time by a curve-fitting routine.

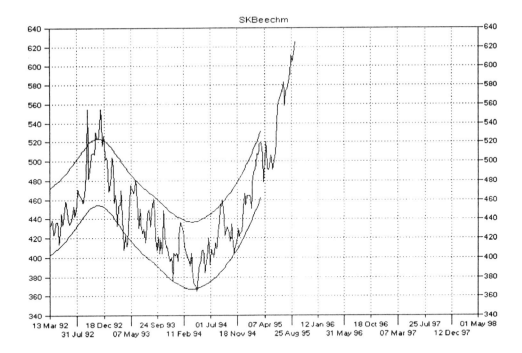

Figure 8.24 When the actual channel is viewed from the future it can be seen that the predicted channel was a good estimate

PROBABILITY METHODS

As we have seen from the many examples so far, the difficulty we face using centred moving averages as templates for channels is the necessity of filling in the gap between the last calculated point and the present day or near future. We depend heavily upon peaks or troughs occurring in this missing section to enable us to take decisions about changes in direction of the channels. The recently developed Sigma-p program uses probability methods to estimate the future course of a long term channel. It also shows where a trend might change direction. A good illustration of its power is if we apply it to the case of SmithKleinBeecham at about the time we used in the previous example. In Figure 8.23 we found that we were unable to predict that the channel was turning until the price rose considerably above the extrapolated channel on 2nd September 1994.

Since Sigma-p predictions do not depend fundamentally on the position of peaks and troughs in this missing section, the program can make a prediction that a channel has changed direction not only much sooner than

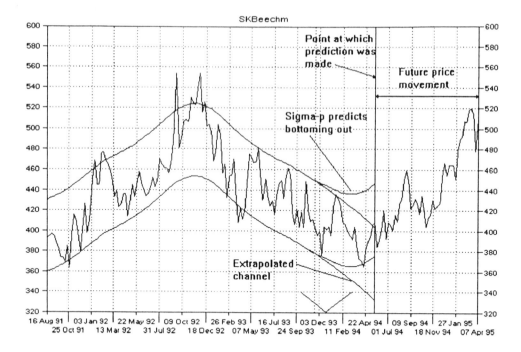

Figure 8.25   The Sigma-p probability program predicts a turn in the channel at a time when the traditional extrapolation shows a slightly increased rate of fall. The prediction is made on 20th May 1994 at the vertical line

the standard method, but **before** it changes direction. In other words it predicts a turn in the channel in advance rather than after the event. The prediction takes the form of a time window in which it is probable that the turn will take place. While the investor should obviously not make an investment in advance of the turn, it means that at the point at which it is predicted, the investor can wait for the appropriate minor troughs and peaks in the share price to point to the exact time for investment.

Figure 8.25 shows the comparison between the traditional method and the Sigma-p method of channel prediction at a point just after the turn occurred. The traditional method is still showing a falling channel, with, if anything, a slight increase in the rate of descent. On the other hand, Sigma-p shows quite clearly the channel turning point, and comparison with Figure 8.24 shows how accurate the prediction was.

The chevron represents a time window where there is an 80% probability that a turn in the long term trend will occur, using a different method of calculation from that employed to estimate the channel. The centre of the chevron is the most likely turning point. A better view of these two predictions is obtained in the enlarged section shown in Figure 8.26.

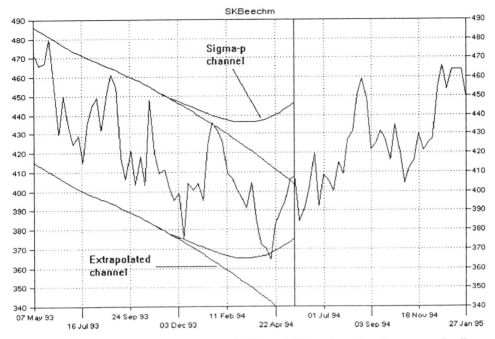

Figure 8.26 The turning point section in Figure 8.25 is enlarged to show more detail

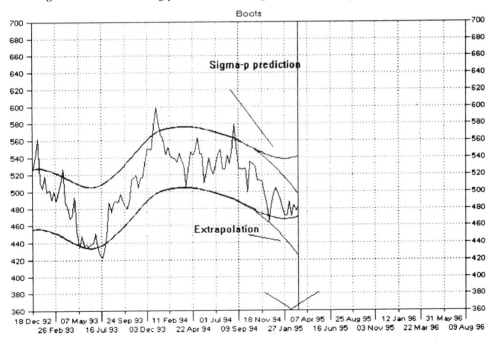

Figure 8.27 The Sigma-p probability program predicts a turn in the channel for Boots at a time when the traditional exptrapolation shows a greatly increased rate of fall

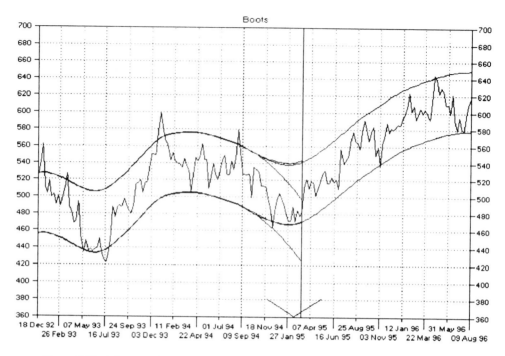

Figure 8.28   The actual channel in Boots viewed from a year later in time, showing the accuracy of the predicted channel at the turning point

Figure 8.27 shows both the estimated channel and the estimated long term trend turning point for Boots as at March 1995. At this point the traditional channel obtained by extrapolation of the calculated channel shows an increased rate of fall, with no indication that a turning point has been reached. The Sigma-p channel, however, shows quite clearly that the bottom has just been passed and that therefore the long term trend is up. The alternative chevron calculation also supports this, showing that we are within the 80% probability turning band.

Figure 8.28 shows a calculation of the actual channel performed a year later in time. The channel calculated by Sigma-p is almost exactly superimposable over the actual one, showing the uncanny accuracy of a prediction made at a time when there was no indication whatsoever that the long term trend would turn up.

Research using Sigma-p has shown that the predictability of the turning points in long term trends in shares varies considerably from one share to another. It is possible to rank shares in a numerical order of predictability so that the investor can ignore shares where predictability is low. This decreases the risk considerably.

9

Maintaining a Pool of Shares

As was pointed out in the first chapter, the objective of any investor should be to maximise the rate at which his investments are gaining. It was also pointed out using Grand Metropolitan shares as an example that a series of short term successful trades, averaging about 12 weeks per trade, compounded into huge gains over the long term. In order to satisfy these two criteria, the investor has to be ready to close his position in a share which is entering the autumn of its rising trend, and immediately move into another share for which spring is just blossoming. As well as maintaining a very close watch on the share or shares in which he is currently invested, the investor therefore has to maintain a watch on these shares from which the next opportunity will arise. This task is vitally important if the momentum of investment is to be kept going. Fortunately for most of the time it does not require quite the constant and extensive analysis that must be applied to the share prices of those investments that are being held. By the time the current investment is appearing to be ready to terminate, then the possible selections should have been reduced to just a few. It is to these few that a great deal of attention then has to be paid in order to select the one share that will carry our hopes for the next stage of our investment. Note the important fact that is stressed in Chapter 10. We should apply no more than an eighth of our capital to any one share. Under no circumstances should we deviate from this rule. It is very rare for the market to pass through situations where the next investment cannot be found. Although the week following the crash of 1987 would have been one of the few times when the investor should have been totally disinvested, a week or so after that he would have been embarrassed by the enormous number of opportunities for making huge gains in a very short period of time.

A list of between 50 and 100 shares is perfectly adequate for most periods in stock market history as a pool from which prime selections can be taken. This list is not static, and as time goes on some shares will be deleted from the pool and new ones brought in. For those investors with computer systems and a database that includes, say, the FTSE100 constituents plus any other shares which are present in the Traded Options list, then maintaining a watching brief on these is a task that takes very little time. For those investors without such a capability, the work necessary to maintain charts of share prices will make it more attractive to minimise the number, keeping this nearer to 50 shares than 100. In order to keep the amount of work to a minimum, it is only necessary to keep track of weekly closing values at this stage. It is only when the moment is approaching for selling your current holding that you could consider moving to daily data on your few prime selections in order to make a final choice, but even this is not vitally important. As we showed in the last chapter, using daily data should normally improve your profit from a trade by a few percentage points, but it is debatable whether the extra amount of work necessary to track daily data rather than weekly data makes this really worthwhile if a computer system is not available.

The major criteria upon which to base your selections for the main pool should be:

- Volatility—good swings in price for all types of cycles, short, medium and long term. This is reflected in a greater depth of the channel encompassing these cycles of interest.
- Good evidence of cyclical behaviour.
- Low amount of random, week-to-week or day-to-day movement.
- Evidence that cycles of less than one year periodicity are not decreasing in importance.
- Troughs in cycles of more than one year periodicity are approaching.

The main requirement for selection from the main pool into the prime pool should be:

- A trough in one or more cycles of less than one year periodicity is approaching. This will allow us to make an investment at the correct time in cycles which will gain the maximum over the typical investment period of 12 weeks.

In order to give a flavour of the appearance of a reasonable number of share price charts, 24 charts are presented here in Figures 9.1–9.24. They are taken from the FTSE100 constituents plus the mid-250 constituents. The timescales are not all the same, since some shares start at an earlier time than others. The scales have been adjusted so as to allow the share movement to fill about half to three-quarters of the width of the chart. **The time axis is marked in weeks rather than with a date**, since this allows the wavelength of various cycles to be more readily obtained. A good enough approximation of the number of years covered by each chart is obtained by dividing the number of weeks to the end of the data by 50 rather than 52. Since the charts all terminate at the same position, in late October 1996, the crash of 1987 is about week 250.

We shall comment on each individual chart, so that you will see which of these would be selected for our main pool. Note that because this selection is made now, at the time of writing, there is no implication that the same shares would be selected for the main pool at some time in the future. The main features of a share which made it a good candidate at a certain point in time will almost certainly change, and next month or next year it might not fulfil the requirements. The main pool must be kept under constant revision.

All the shares are on a rising trend at the time of writing. In a broad sense therefore the shares are behaving similarly.

A closer look at the various charts does show up a difference when it comes to short term random movements. Some shares have an obviously greater random content than others. On the scale of the charts, which are covering periods of up to just over 700 weeks, the fine detail of this random movement is not discernible. The presence of such random movement is indicated by a fuzziness of the share price movement. These shares are never standing still, and an investor monitoring the movement on a day-to-day basis will nearly always see a change in price. As two extreme examples, compare the random week-to-week movement of British Telecom (Figure 9.6) with the much lesser movement in Dixons (Figure 9.8). Note also that a share can change character over a number of years, from a low amount of random short-term movement to a much larger amount or vice versa. An example of this is Standard Chartered (Figure 9.21). Although in general we should ignore shares in which the day-to-day or week-to-week random movement is high, we can make an exception where there are particularly strong cycles present.

Moving on to slightly longer cycles than the random movement, we should notice that the fuzziness in the GUS share price (Figure 9.12), for example, is not as densely packed as in some other shares, the reason being that the GUS share price contains a great deal of short-term cyclical movement in addition to a small amount of random movement. For a good example of short term cyclical movement uncluttered by too much random movement, the Land Securities price (Figure 9.14) between weeks 300 and 500 is an excellent example. Again, the principle of variation in amplitude of cycles is well illustrated, since these short term cycles have disappeared between weeks 500 and 600. Good examples of shares which have maintained their short term cyclical behaviour are Pilkington (Figure 9.16) and W.H. Smith (Figure 9.20).

These comments so far should lead you to the conclusion that although there has been some underlying upwards momentum given to the vast majority of shares over the last five to ten years, each share has its own character, although each share's character is undergoing change. Some shares are very random, some show short term cyclical behaviour, some medium term cyclical behaviour, some long term cyclical behaviour, and some show mixtures of some or all of these effects. In some shares the combination of many of these effects puts them in a favourable position for investment almost immediately, while in others the opposite is the case.

It is useful to categorise the shares by awarding them from one to three stars for increasing prominence of random and cyclical movement. The cyclical movement can be subdivided into very short term, say up to 20 weeks' periodicity, short term from over 20 weeks to about one year, medium term from over one year to just over two years, and long term over two years. It is not necessary to spend a great deal of time doing this, and a rapid impression of the various cycles can be obtained by looking at the distances between successive troughs of waves of good amplitude. The most recent history is the most important, and if a cycle which was present at the start of the chart is not apparent at the end of the chart, which in every case is October 1996, then it should be given only one star. It is not intended that the trough-to-trough distances are measured accurately, but just mentally put into the appropriate time slots. Draw a channel in your mind's eye to accommodate these fluctuations. The very approximate depth of the channel in pence which you can get from this exercise can be used to grade the amplitude of the various cycles to award a star rating. The deeper the channel, the greater the potential for profit from a share price move from the lower boundary to the upper boundary, and therefore the greater the star rating. You may wish to see if you obtain similar results to those shown in Table 9.1. You may not agree entirely with these, since in a rapid scan such as this a certain amount of subjectivity prevails. The most important objective of this rapid scan is to draw our attention to those shares which are worth a more detailed analysis.

As can be seen from the table, most of the charts merit only one star for their long term cyclicality of over two years' periodicity. The use of this column is more to draw attention to the very few shares that achieve two or three stars. These will offer above average opportunities at some time in the future when the long term cycle bottoms out and happens to coincide with an upswing in shorter cycles. For immediate investment the long term cyclicality is of little importance.

Some of the shares can be eliminated immediately from our pool on the grounds of general lack of cyclicality. These are BOC, GUS, Hillsdown, Standard Chartered and Thorn-EMI (Figures 9.4, 9.12, 9.13, 9.21 and 9.22). This does not mean of course that we cannot make profits in these shares. It is simply that for our purposes we can find very much better vehicles for investment in the remainder of the shares in our list.

Some shares are outstanding for their mixture of all types of periodicity, for example Land Securities, Pilkington and United Biscuits (Figures 9.14, 9.16 and 9.24). These must be prime candidates for a much more detailed analysis, remaining on our list for a long time to come even if the analysis shows that they are not immediate investment opportunities. Even though they do not merit two stars in the long term cycle column, then since we have said that this is of little consequence, we can add Bass, British Telecom, General Accident, Legal & General, Reckitt & Colman, Redland

Table 9.1 Strong cycles present in leading shares. Cycles are graded on a one to three star basis, one star being weak and three stars strong

	Cycles				
	Random movement	Up to 20 weeks	20 weeks to 1 year	1 year to 2 years	Over 2 years
1 Abbey National	**	**	**	*	*
2 Barclays	*	**	***	***	*
3 Bass	*	***	***	***	*
4 BOC	*	**	**	*	*
5 British Airways	**	**	**	**	*
6 British Telecom	**	***	***	***	*
7 Cable & Wireless	*	**	***	***	*
8 Dixons	*	***	**	**	**
9 General Accident	*	***	***	***	*
10 Glaxo-Wellcome	*	*	***	***	*
11 Guardian Royal	**	***	***	***	*
12 GUS	**	**	*	*	*
13 Hillsdown	**	***	*	*	**
14 Land Securities	*	***	***	***	**
15 Legal & General	**	***	***	***	*
16 Pilkington	**	***	***	***	**
17 Reckitt & Colman	**	***	***	***	*
18 Redland	**	***	***	***	*
19 Rolls-Royce	**	***	**	**	*
20 W.H. Smith	**	***	***	**	*
21 Standard Chartered	*	**	**	**	*
22 Thorn-EMI	*	***	**	*	*
23 Unigate	**	***	***	***	*
24 United Biscuits	**	***	***	***	**

and Unigate (Figures 9.3, 9.6, 9.9, 9.15, 9.17, 9.18 and 9.23), since all of their other cycles are featured strongly.

Our investment objective is to concentrate on cycles of up to one year's periodicity, which means cycles where the trough-to-peak rise time is up to 26 weeks. As discussed for the Grand Metropolitan case (Chapter 1) we aim to stay invested on average for about 12 weeks in any one share, so shares which have three stars in both the column for cycles up to 20 weeks and the column for cycles from 20 weeks to one year are of interest. This will give us a manageable number of 10 shares. These are Bass, British Telecom, General Accident, Land Securities, Legal & General, Pilkington, Reckitt & Colman, Redland, Unigate and United Biscuits.

Since these shares contain a variety of cycles from very short wavelengths up to one year, we will be able to aim for situations where two or even three cycles are about to reach their troughs. As we have stated earlier, when this happens, the upward momentum given to the share price is additive, consisting of the sum of the rises that each of the two or more components would make over the following few weeks individually.

Conversely, of course, any longer term cycle that is about to fall from that point in time will have an adverse effect, subtracting from the rise that would otherwise be made. The longer the periodicity of this adverse cycle, the shallower is its fall, so that over a short term of a few weeks or months, it may not fall very much. It is for this reason that, although it is extremely useful to be able to time an investment when a longer term cycle of say four years or more is about to bottom out, its effect over a few weeks or months is usually not very large, and in the opposite sense of shorter term cycles dictating that an investment be made the negative effect of such a long term cycle topping out should be ignored. A good illustration of this is the Reckitt & Colman share price (Figure 9.17). An obvious outer channel is going through a very long term top. Even so, the depth of this channel is such that price rises within it will show considerable gains of 30% or more if good timing is achieved. If this approach is not made, the investor will be forced into the position of being dictated to by the longer term cycles in the market, and will not begin to approach the gains we discussed in Chapter 1.

Having now reduced our original 24 shares down to 10, they should be analysed carefully by the techniques of channel analysis and moving averages. Readers may care to transfer these charts to tracing paper and draw channels on the traces. It is permissible to draw as many channels as you like until the outer channel is reached, as long as each channel is enclosed by another one such as to obey the rules about channel construction mentioned in earlier chapters. It is unlikely on the amount of data presented in these figures that more than four such nested channels can be drawn, and probably two channels will be adequate for most of the charts. Even without doing this, it is still possible to make some brief, preliminary observations about the investment potential of each of these shares at the time of writing (25th October 1996) as follows:

Bass (Figure 9.3)

The 53-week channel appears to have just topped out by virtue of hitting the upper boundary of a very long term channel. The price is now at the bottom of the 53-week channel, and can be expected to bounce up to the upper boundary, giving a potential profit of about 70p. Once this short term movement is over, the share will be one to avoid for some time to come.

British Telecom (Figure 9.6)

The 53-week channel has just passed its low point, with the price having fallen to the newly rising lower boundary. A trough is yet to be formed, but once one has been formed at the boundary, this should be the start of a good rise of 70p at the very least.

General Accident (Figure 9.9)

The price has just risen dramatically and is now at the upper boundary which is still rising. It is now too late to buy into the share, but it would be held until a stop loss penetration (see Chapter 10) signals time to exit.

Land Securities (Figure 9.14)

The price bounced off the lower boundary of the 53-week channel some weeks back. It is now too late to buy into this share, but we would expect a rise of about 50p or so before a stop loss is triggered.

Legal & General (Figure 9.15)

This is a case where insurance shares have all behaved in unison. The comments above for General Accident apply in exactly the same way for Legal & General.

Pilkington (Figure 9.16)

The 53-week channel has topped out, and the price is now falling towards the lower boundary which is itself now falling. The share should have been sold many weeks ago as a stop loss would have been triggered. It is unlikely that a buying point will occur for the best part of a year from the present time.

Reckitt & Colman (Figure 9.17)

There are signs that the 53-week channel is topping out, with the price now approaching the upper boundary. Certainly not a buying position, but if the share is held there might be a further small rise to be obtained as the price makes a last effort to reach the upper boundary. It would have to be watched very carefully with a stop loss in order to exit at the first sign of an adverse trend.

Redland (Figure 9.18)

The channel is rising strongly, with the price some way above the lower boundary. We would have to wait for a small fall towards the lower boundary with the formation of a trough, at which time there will be a good buying opportunity. A substantial rise should follow.

Unigate (Figure 9.23)

In this case the channel has almost certainly topped out, with the price at the upper boundary. Expect a fall from this point. It will be a long time before this share shows a good buying signal.

United Biscuits (Figure 9.24)

The channel is falling rapidly, with the price contained in the middle of it. It is impossible to predict from the present data when the channel will stop falling. The share should not be bought until a turnaround is fully substantiated.

These comments about the 10 shares should serve to show the features we are looking for when determining if a share is to be a good investment almost immediately, in the near future, or perhaps not for some consider-able time in the future. As you have more practice in looking at more charts, you will get to a position when just a glance at a share price chart will enable you to decide whether it is useless for current investment purposes or worth a much more detailed analysis.

Always adopt the view that if you are not sure whether a particular share is at the right point in its development to be considered to be the next investment opportunity, then there will always be another share about which you can be sure. If you cannot find such an alternative im-mediately, then wait until you can, rather than invest in a situation in which you do not have 100% faith that you are making the correct investment.

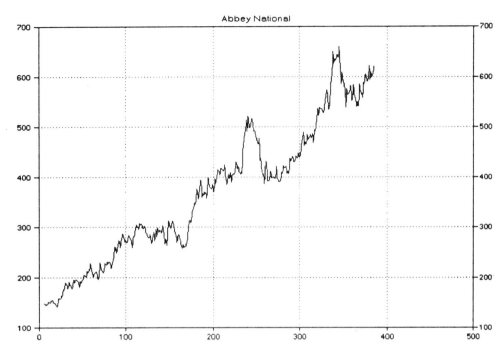

Figure 9.1 Abbey National share price

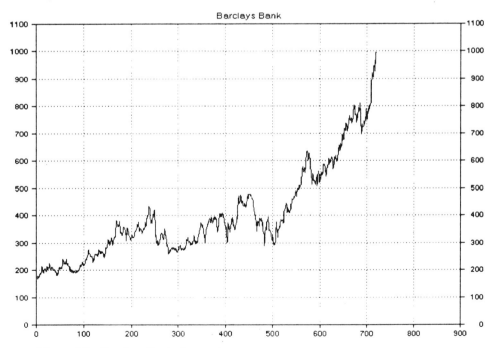

Figure 9.2 Barclays Bank share price

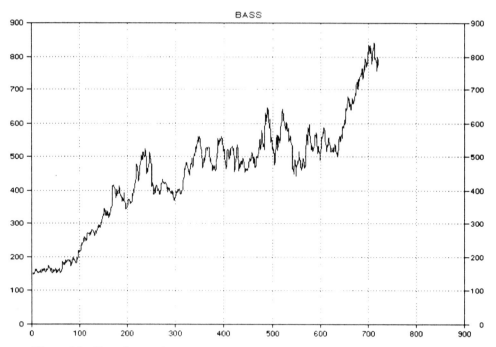

Figure 9.3 Bass share price

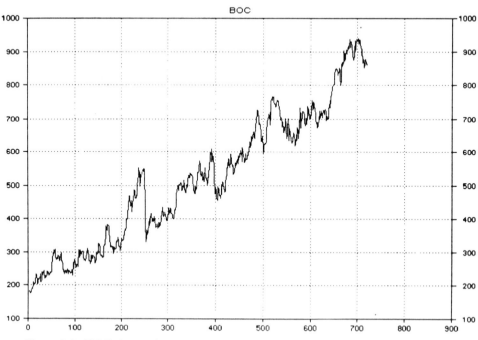

Figure 9.4 BOC share price

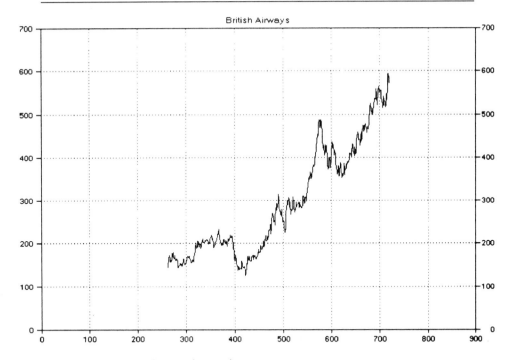

Figure 9.5   British Airways share price

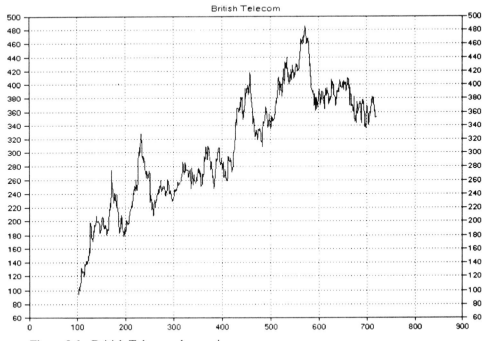

Figure 9.6   British Telecom share price

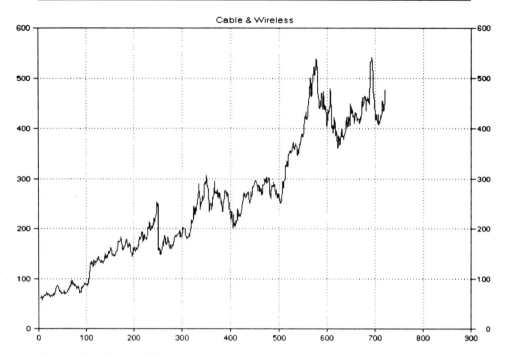

Figure 9.7   Cable & Wireless share price

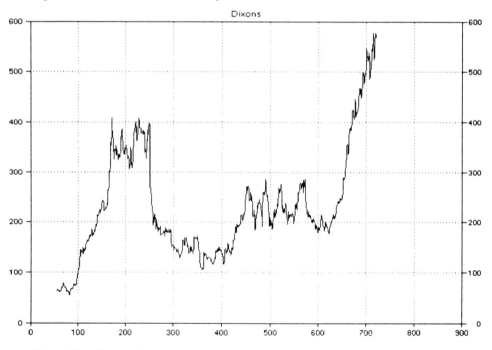

Figure 9.8   Dixons share price

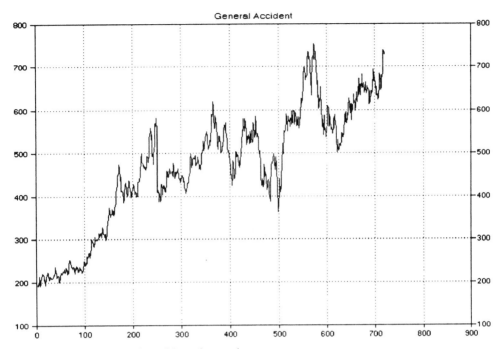

Figure 9.9 General Accident share price

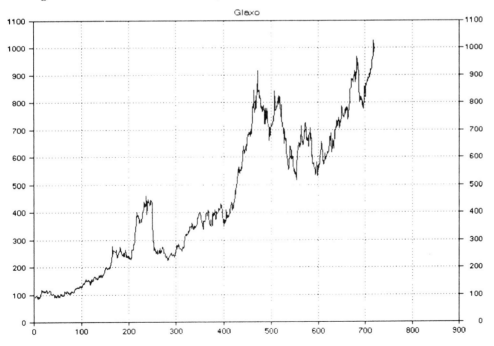

Figure 9.10 Glaxo-Wellcome share price

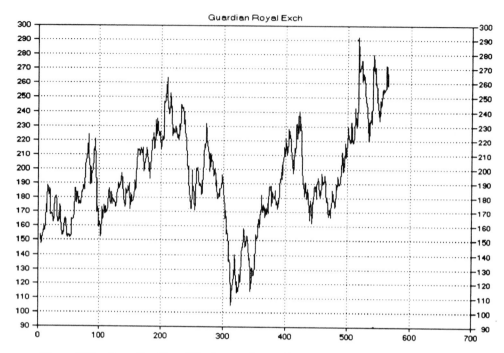

Figure 9.11   Guardian Royal Exchange share price

Figure 9.12   GUS share price

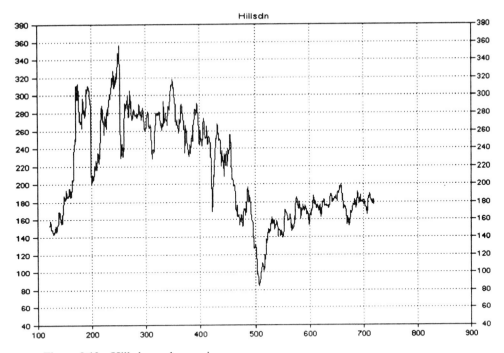

Figure 9.13   Hillsdown share price

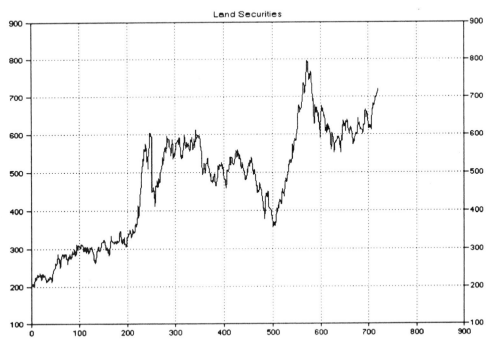

Figure 9.14   Land Securities share price

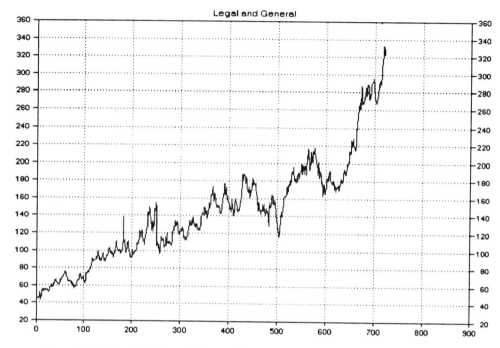

Figure 9.15   Legal & General share price

Figure 9.16   Pilkington share price

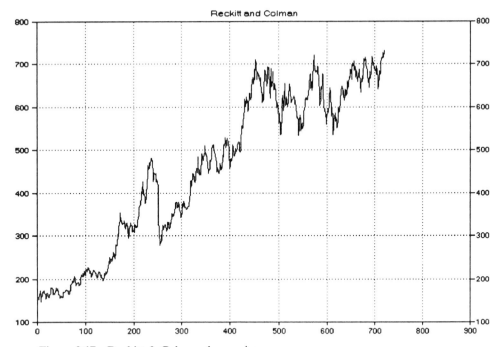

Figure 9.17 Reckitt & Colman share price

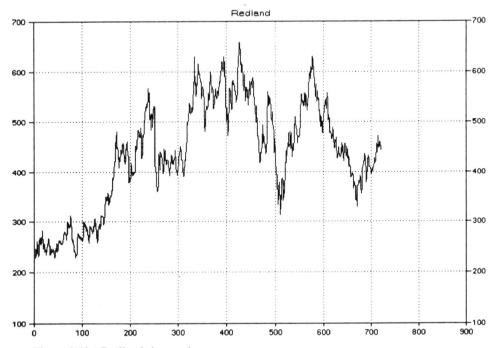

Figure 9.18 Redland share price

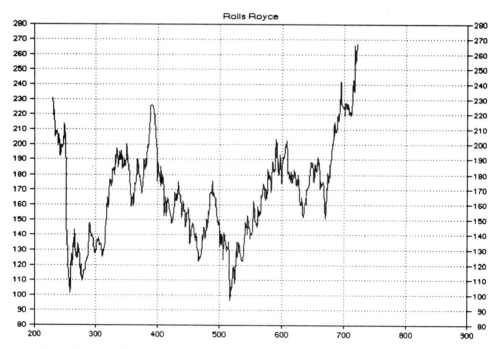

Figure 9.19 Rolls-Royce share price

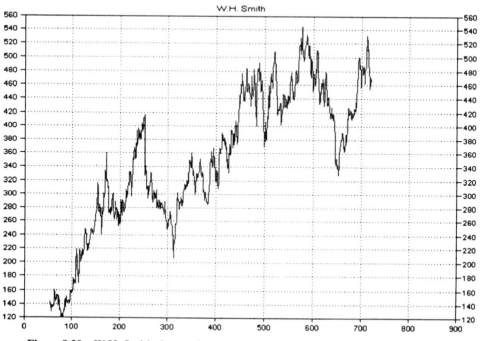

Figure 9.20 W.H. Smith share price

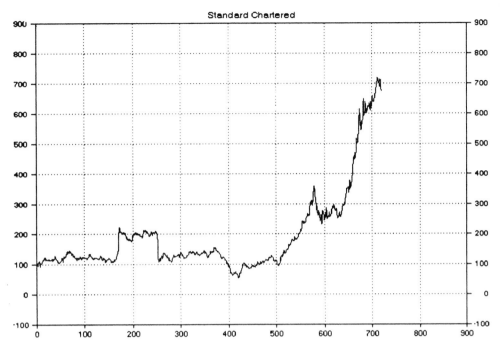

Figure 9.21 Standard Chartered share price

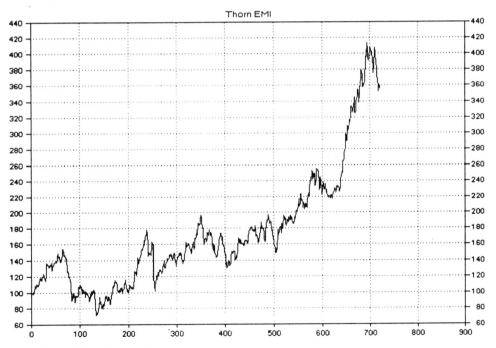

Figure 9.22 Thorn-EMI share price

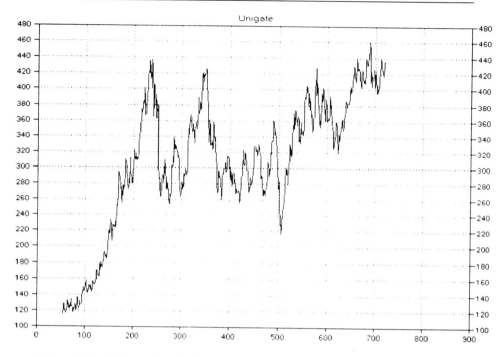

Figure 9.23   Unigate share price

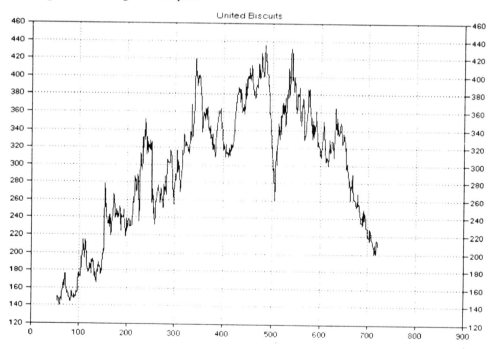

Figure 9.24   United Biscuits shared price

10

Staying Disciplined

The laws of probability are such that as more transactions are carried out, the results approach the ideal ever more closely. Thus the tossing of an evenly balanced coin may result in five or even more consecutive heads being produced, but if the coin is tossed 1000 times, the results will be close to the theoretical 500 heads and 500 tails. So it is with the techniques and methods discussed in this book, which stand the test of time. We do not claim that the methods are foolproof and consistently predict the turning points in share price trends. We have constantly pointed out that the random content of share price movement is totally unpredictable, but taken over a reasonable number of transactions, these techniques move the balance of probabilities substantially in favour of the investor. Taken over just one or two transactions, the results may not go the way that the investor would like. The way in which investors lose money is to fail to admit that they have made a mistake, and thereby fail to cut short a losing position early on before substantial losses have accumulated. If investors can overcome this psychological problem, they shift the balance of probabilities even more in their favour, because they will allow their profits to run while minimising their losses. Failure to maintain discipline at all times will totally negate the powerful techniques which have been presented in this book. Some guideline rules which should help the investor to maintain this discipline are presented in the following pages. Most of these rules are a natural consequence of paying attention to the laws of probability.

CAPITAL MUST BE PRESERVED AT ALL COSTS

This is the first and overriding rule of stock market investment, and the remaining rules and comments are designed so that this first rule can be followed consistently. The natural consequence of this rule is that when a position has been taken in a share, the investor must get out as soon as it is obvious that the share price is misbehaving. There will always be another opportunity for making profit. The prevention of loss is as important as the achievement of profit. Remember, there is no such thing as a paper loss. All losses are real.

NEVER ACT SOLELY ON ADVICE

Besides the internal pressure to stray from this disciplined path caused by investor psychology, the external pressures from the investment industry are immense. The investor is constantly bombarded with advice from stockbrokers, junk mail and the media.

Some of the most successful investors read nothing but the share prices page in their newspaper and do not even glance at the rest of the business section. I would not go quite as far as this, since a feel for the general investment climate which can be gained from these pages can be extremely valuable. By all means listen to advice from whatever source, but never, never act on it without analysing the data by the methods discussed in this book and then act only if the analysis is favourable.

NEVER PUT MORE THAN ONE-EIGHTH OF YOUR CAPITAL IN ONE SHARE

However positively the investor feels about the potential for a particular share, this positive feeling must be tempered by knowledge of the existence of random movement. Because of this, the investor should not, and must not, have 100% confidence in any one given situation. The temptation to go for broke and put everything into one magic share is always at the back of the investor's mind, and that is where it should stay. Never, never commit more than one-eighth of the investment capital to one share. This will keep the risk as low as possible while maintaining the potential for profit. From time to time there will be occasions when it is not possible to find eight shares in which to invest. In such cases put the money into short term interest-bearing accounts where it can be got at instantly when the need arises.

DO NOT PREDICT TOO FAR AHEAD

We have pointed out that the uncertainty of prediction increases rapidly as we move further and further into the future. It is not necessary to look further ahead than about three to six months.

In Chapter 1 we showed that substantial profits could be made in trends of about three months' duration. When we are rapidly approaching a buying point, a three- to six-month horizon is more than adequate.

DO NOT ANTICIPATE SHARE PRICE TURNING POINTS

A close attention to Chapter 9 and the discussion of market turning points will show that we should never anticipate a turning point. We should never make an investment until after the change in direction of the trend has been confirmed, and we should never disinvest until the change in direction has been confirmed. Channel analysis will tell us the approximate time and approximate price level of approaching turning points. This enables us to focus closely on what is happening, constantly updating and fine tuning the channels as mini-troughs and peaks are formed. As each trough and peak confirms our prediction of the direction of the channels, we gain in confidence that we will recognise the change in direction a very short time after it occurs. The profit available in upward trends which we buy into shortly after the start of these new trends is such that we do not need to worry about squeezing an extra one or two percentage points out by trying to anticipate them.

PROTECT PROFITS BY STOP LOSSES

Just as it is not necessary to try to squeeze extra gain out of a trend by jumping the gun, so it is not necessary to try to squeeze extra gain by continuing to run after the finishing tape has been passed. In the majority of cases, the termination of an upward trend results in a sudden sharp reversal of price over the course of one or two days. The risk increases dramatically as the inner channel increases in upward slope. Although we have shown by channel analysis that we can determine the selling point closely in time, it is essential that we protect ourselves against the conjunction of an adverse random movement and a change in direction of short term cycles.

The most common stop loss method is based on percentages. This will generate a selling signal that is a consistent percentage down from the peak price. The method is a rigid one, with no room for subjective interpretation, and therefore will have its failures in the sense of premature selling. Its advantage is that it is extremely simple to use, so that no interpretive effort has to be expended once a buying decision has been taken. On the other hand, investors using it will never have the expensive failure of seeing the price fall dramatically before action is taken.

The stop loss method is based on having a "floor price", with a fall of the share price below this floor being the signal to sell. As the share price rises, the floor price is raised to keep a constant distance below it. The floor is not moved when the price falls, otherwise of course the price would never fall below it. There are two main variations on the method. In the first, the floor is kept a fixed percentage below the rising price and raised with every upward share price movement. In the second, the floor is kept a fixed number of pence below the rising price and again raised with every upward share price movement.

Any stop loss system has two diametrically opposed requirements, which are to protect the investor against a fall in price, but not to cause the investor to sell too soon, since share prices obviously fluctuate up and down as the underlying trend is rising. A stop loss which is only a small price differential below the rising share price will cause the investor to be "stopped out", i.e. to sell his shares much too frequently, thus consistently losing the profit from the share price which continues to rise after a minor hiccup. Such a stop loss protects the investor against even small falls, but at the expense of profit. On the other hand, a stop loss which is a long way below the share price will allow profitable situations to run, but will also allow large falls to develop before being triggered. Conservative investors should use a small differential while more aggressive ones can use a wider differential.

Percentage Stop Losses

The best position for a percentage stop loss can only be determined by trial and error on a number of share prices, until a value is obtained that keeps the investor in for the majority of good rises and still allows him to make an acceptable profit. A value around 3% or 4% will be found to be useful for the majority of shares. Thus, on balance, the investors who take the trouble to analyse channel movement carefully during large price rises will do better than those who use a stop loss, but the users of the latter will have a simple method which requires very little effort.

Fixed Amount Stop Losses

The method of using a constant price in pence below the rising price is more in tune with channel analysis, because channel analysis is concerned not with percentage movement but with absolute movement. This is why all channels must have a constant depth. With a percentage-based method, the channel depth would get larger the higher the price rises, and narrower as it falls. Besides being almost impossible to draw such channels by a freehand method, the fact is that such a method does not work for channels.

Since the main idea of the analysis is to avoid selling on a price fall which is only due to random movement, but sell when the underlying cycles start to move adversely, then the level at which we pitch the constant floor below the rising price should bear a relationship to the depth of the innermost channel that can be drawn, i.e. the channel that contains these random fluctuations. It is suggested that a value of half of the depth of the channel be used. Since at areas near to the peak tops the inner channel will be rising at a sharp angle, half of the channel depth represents a considerable fall back from the upper boundary.

The method of placing a floor half of a channel depth below the price can be seen to give similar results to those obtained by a careful analysis of the price movement where the price falling below the lower boundary of the inner channel is the signal to sell. Again, the point can be made that using the floor is very much easier than a detailed channel analysis, but cannot approach the good results obtained by looking for a bounce back from the channel upper boundary.

PROTECT AGAINST LOSSES BY STOP LOSSES

This would appear to mean the same as the previous heading, but here we mean the stop loss to apply not to the profitable position above, but to the case where an incorrect buying decision has been made and the share starts to fall in price instead of rising. In this case the position never was in profit. Even so, the rule about protection of capital is paramount. The temptation is to think that we were slightly premature in recognising the start of the upward trend, and that in a few more days or weeks the expected trend will materialise. This attitude is a major cause of stock market losses, and must never be adopted. Use the same stop loss procedures as we discussed for profitable situations in Chapter 9. Never forget that if we can reduce our losses to say 4% or 5%, including dealing costs, when we make a bad decision, then this is only 4% or 5% of one-eighth of our total capital. We can afford to experience theoretically 20 to 25 such losses before one-eighth of our capital is wiped out, and 160 to 200 such losses before we are totally wiped out. The chances of this happening are at vanishing point for the conservative investment philosophy policy we are advocating in this book.

STAY WITH TOP SHARES

In Chapter 1 we showed the crucial influence of dealing costs on profit. The spread of prices, i.e. the difference between buying and selling prices for a share, is part of this equation. The spread is at a minimum for a share which is a constituent of the FTSE100 Index, and slightly more for constituents of the mid-250 Index. This gives 350 shares in all, and there is usually plenty of opportunity for finding a share amongst these which is approaching an upward trend.

IGNORE DIVIDENDS

Dividends are nice to receive, and if the investor is fully invested in eight different shares for most of the year, he can expect to receive many dividends which will add to his profit. That is all that can be said about them, for the investor should never let an impending dividend affect his buying or selling operation. In other words, if the signal comes to sell, do not think of hanging on for a little longer because the dividend will be announced the following week. If a buying point is approaching, do not buy in before the change in direction is confirmed simply because a dividend will be captured.

KEEP TRACK OF THE MARKET

It is always essential that the general investment climate is tracked by means of a market indicator such as the FT30 Index, the FT All Share Index or the FTSE100 Index. Weekly values are sufficient to do this, and channels can be drawn on the charts just as in the case of shares in order to get a feel for the direction of the market. In view of the increasing tendency of London to follow slavishly the gyrations of Wall Street, it is also a good idea to keep track of the Dow Jones Index on a weekly basis. Short term dramatic movements in the US market almost always cause an effect in the London market.

If the market is falling, adopt a more cautious stance towards your existing holdings and new purchases, and watch your stop losses very carefully.

The investor may well find that in the initial stages it is very difficult to stick to this investment philosophy. He may find that straying off this narrow path brings him an instant reward that he would otherwise have missed. This is just the quixotic nature of the world of probability. Over a number of years the investor following these guidelines will see his capital gaining steadily in value, while the investor who allows himself to be diverted from time to time will be subjecting himself to increasing risk that will inevitably take its toll.

Finally, the investor who has successfully followed these techniques for perhaps a year or so will begin to look for greater gains than those which can be made out of investment in shares. Then, and not before, is the time to turn to the magnifying effect of dealing in traded options. In inexperienced hands traded options can be unacceptably risky, but they can be extremely rewarding when they are thoroughly understood and when the investor is correct about the movement of the underlying security. The author's previous book *Traded Options Simplified* will take the beginner from the basics through to simple strategies and then on to advanced strategies, as well as discussing some powerful new techniques for investors familiar with the field.

Appendix

Addresses

For lists of brokers: The Secretary, The International Stock Exchange of the United Kingdom and the Republic of Ireland Ltd, The Stock Exchange, London EC2N 1HP

Previous Editions by the Author

Stocks and Shares Simplified (3rd edn), ISBN 0-471-92131-9, published by John Wiley & Sons Ltd, Chichester.

Traded Options Simplified (1st edn), ISBN 1-871857-00-7, published by Qudos Publications, distributed by John Wiley & Sons Ltd, Chichester.

Channel Analysis (1st edn), ISBN 1-871857-02-3, published by Qudos Publications, distributed by John Wiley & Sons Ltd, Chichester.

Winning on the Stock Market (1st edn), ISBN 0-471-93881-5, published by John Wiley & Sons Ltd, Chichester.

Profitable Charting Techniques (1st edn), ISBN 1-871857-03-1, published by Qudos Publications, distributed by John Wiley & Sons Ltd, Chichester.

Historical Data

Weekly closing prices of shares since 1982 are obtainable in printed form (ISBN 1-871857-01-5) or on floppy disk from:
Qudos Publications, PO Box 27, Bramhall, Stockport, Cheshire SK7 1JH
Tel. 0161 439 3926
Fax 0161 439 2327

Microcomputer Software

The charts in this book were produced by the Microvest 5.0 and Sigma-p packages published by Qudos Publications Ltd.

Index